OTHER TITLES IN THE SERIES

Alternative Kilns
Ian Gregory

Ceramics with Mixed Media
Joy Bosworth

Ceramics and Print
Paul Scott

Coiling
Michael Hardy

Colouring Clay
Jo Connell

Crystalline Glazes
Diane Creber

Dry Glazes
Jeremy Jernegan

The Electric Kiln
Harry Fraser

Glazes Cone 6
Michael Bailey

Handbuilding
Michael Hardy

Paper Clay
Rosette Gault

Porcelain
Jack Doherty

Resist and Masking Techniques
Peter Beard

Slipcasting
Sasha Wardell

Stoneware
Richard Dewar

Soda Glazing
Ruthanne Tudball

Throwing Pots
Phil Rogers

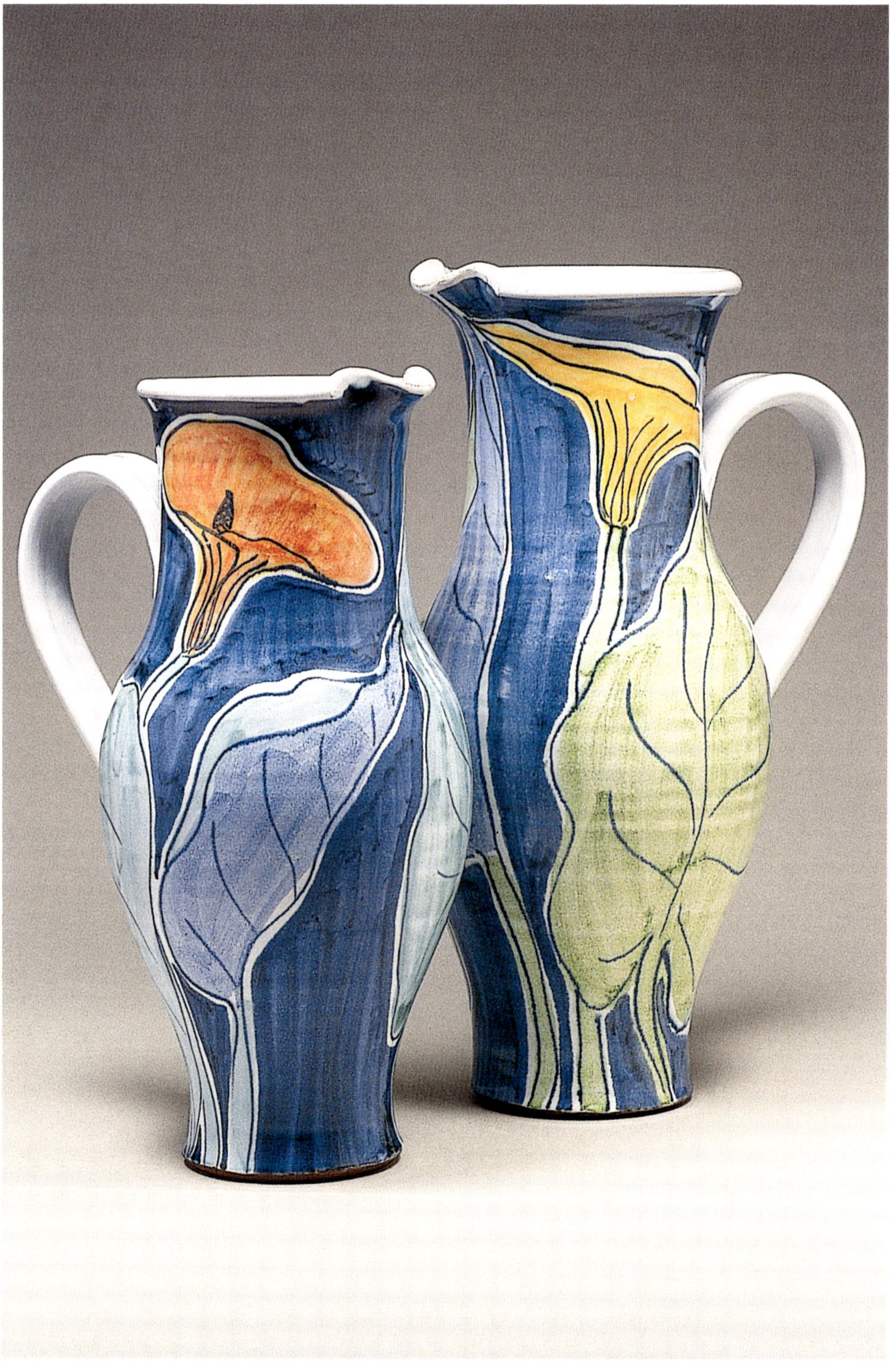

MAIOLICA

Daphne Carnegy

A & C Black • London

University of Pennsylvania Press • Philadelphia

Dedication

For Theo

COVER (FRONT) Vases by Daphne Carnegy, 2009. Ht (tallest): 38 cm (15 in.). *Photo by Sussie Ahlburg.*
COVER (BACK) Dish and jug by Daphne Carnegy, 2004. Dia (dish): 38 cm (15 in.). *Photo by Stephen Brayne.*
FRONTISPIECE Jugs by Daphne Carnegy, 2004. Ht (tallest): 36 cm (14 in.). *Photo by Stephen Brayne.*

First published in Great Britain in 2011
A & C Black Publishers Limited
36 Soho Square
London W1D 3QY
www.acblack.com

ISBN 978-1-408-11416-2

Published simultaneously in the USA by
University of Pennsylvania Press
3905 Spruce Street
Philadelphia, Pennsylvania 19104-4112

ISBN 978-0-8122-2165-7

CIP Catalogue records for this book are available from the British Library and the US Library of Congress.

Typeset in 10 on 12.5pt Photina
Book design by Susan McIntyre
Cover design by Sutchinda Thompson

Printed and bound in Singapore.

This book is produced using paper that is made from wood grown in managed, sustainable forests. It is natural, renewable and recyclable. The logging and manufacturing processes conform to the environmental regulations of the country of origin.

Contents

Acknowledgements

I would like to thank all those maiolica practitioners, friends and family who gave so generously of their contributions and support. Without you, this book would not have been possible. My thanks also go to Linda Lambert and Alison Stace who gave me the opportunity to write the book in the first place!

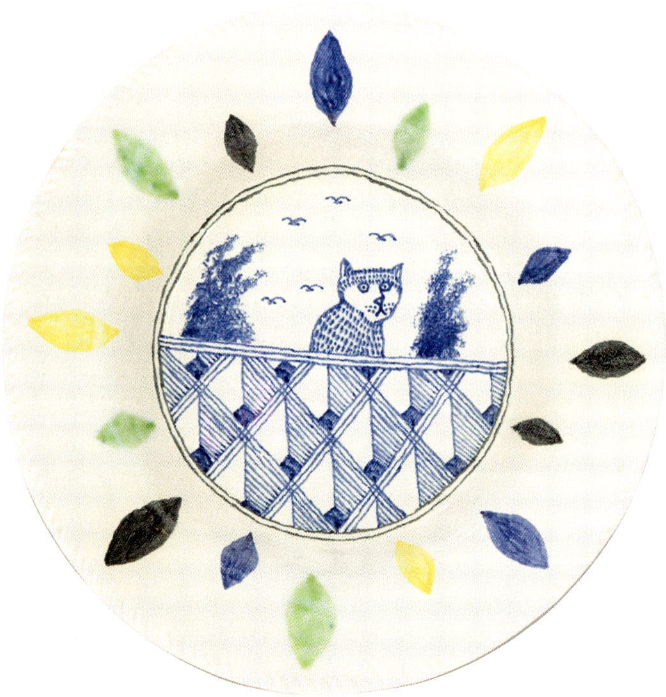

Cat and Trellis plate by Hylton Nel, 2010. Dia: 26 cm (10¼ in.). *Courtesy of Michael Stevenson, Cape Town.*

Introduction

An apprenticeship in France and several visits to Italy introduced me to the delights of earthenware and, in particular, slipware and tin glaze. The late William Newland, himself a supreme champion of both mediums, spoke of earthenware as the sprightly 'Mozart' of ceramics – in contrast to stoneware as the heavyweight 'Beethoven'. The attraction of maiolica for me lies in its unique qualities: a softness, depth and luminosity of glaze and colour not to be found in other ceramic techniques; the transformation of the pigments during firing; and the variations of pigment intensity and texture as they fuse and shift with the glaze. The many variable elements – body, glaze and pigment thickness, along with firing temperature – all conspire to create continual surprises (sometimes good, sometimes not so good) on opening the kiln.

Maiolica was, and still is, a challenge on several levels. Technically, this involves coordinating the many variable elements involved, including bodies, glazes, pigments and firing. Aesthetically, there's the quest for some sort of individual and contemporary expression through brushwork. Finally, there was prejudice – when I first started making in the 1980s, maiolica was generally considered to be 'folksy' and lightweight. Having been a poor relation for such a long time, attitudes have now changed, and maiolica is continually reinventing itself within the world of post-modern contemporary ceramics.

The essence of maiolica involves the use of a white opaque glaze on an earthenware body. What is special about the process is that the pigments – colouring oxides and stains – are traditionally applied to the unfired surface of the glaze, and then become fused with the glaze during the subsequent glaze firing. The technical term for this process is 'in-glaze decoration'. The very whiteness of the glaze, like a canvas, also provides great potential for colour. This makes maiolica a medium which lends itself to a wide variety of surface treatment – both traditional and innovative. This book describes the basic materials, techniques and processes involved with maiolica. It also gives a brief overview of the medium's historical context, and addresses some of the many contemporary approaches to and applications of maiolica; the book is not only intended as a practical handbook of processes and techniques, but is also meant to be a showcase for some of the great variety of work currently being made.

Some of the technical information covered is drawn, in revised form, from aspects of my first book, *Tin-Glazed Earthenware* – since the rudimentary ceramic materials and processes are essentially timeless. On a similar note, I have also made an effort to include valuable material, recipes etc. which continue to remain useful and relevant. However, the focus of this book is concerned with what can be done with maiolica today – emphasising the broad range of contemporary applications and approaches which are currently associated with the medium.

Terminology

I feel that some explanation is required as to the choice of title, and also to clarify the common confusion regarding the various names given to this medium – tin-glazed earthenware, maiolica, majolica, faience, and delftware.

The word 'maiolica' historically refers to tin-glazed earthenware of the Italian Renaissance. However, most North American and many other contemporary practitioners use the word *maiolica* to designate both the process of in-glaze painting on a tin or zirconium-opacified glaze and the resultant wares. The word is also spelt by some as 'majolica' (although strictly speaking, this is a name better reserved to designate the range of coloured, but not tin-glazed ware developed by Mintons in the 1840s). Other historical terms for the medium of tin-glazed earthenware are *faience* (in France and some other European countries), *Delftware* (in the Netherlands) and *English Delftware*.

When deciding on a title for the book, 'tin-glazed earthenware', whilst appropriately used by many practitioners to describe their work, no longer seemed to be entirely accurate as an over-reaching title, since many makers choose to opacify their glazes with the cheaper and sometimes more advantageous zirconium silicate in preference or in addition to tin oxide. As both practice and product are commonly referred to as *maiolica*, this led to the title as it now stands.

Without becoming over-complicated, I have found it necessary to reflect the diversity which exists in the medium's composition and naming. Thus, the terms *maiolica* and *tin-glazed earthenware* are both used in their appropriate historical contexts. Where contemporary work is concerned, these terms are used fairly interchangeably to describe the practice and products of low-temperature tin and/or zircon-opacified glazes. The term *majolica* is only used where the practitioner has himself or herself used this terminology, and it is quoted in either a recipe title or a description.

Cones and temperatures

Cone numbers have been used wherever possible. These refer to Orton regular large cones which can be read off on the chart on p.102. Where only temperatures are given, these are provided in both Celsius and Fahrenheit. In either case, it is strongly recommended that glaze recipes be tested to establish the correct firing rate and temperature to suit your particular requirements.

Chapter 1

A brief history of tin-glazed earthenware

It is extraordinary to think that the whole decorative tradition of tin-glazed earthenware, which came to dominate European ceramics from the early Renaissance until the advent of Josiah Wedgwood's whitewares in the mid-18th century, had its origins in 9th century Mesopotamia. It began as an adventurous imitation of Chinese porcelain and derived its exuberant character from the innate Islamic love of colour and pattern.

The first experiments were carried out under the patronage of the Abbasid Caliphate. These were in emulation of the highly valued Chinese T'ang dynasty porcelain which was being imported into Mesopotamia at the time. These fine wares had been a revelation to the local craftsmen – opening their eyes to the aesthetic potential of pottery. A demand began to grow from the court and the ruling classes for fine and sophisticated wares which the craftsmen were quick to exploit, and new workshops were established under the patronage of the court.

Without access to high-firing white porcellaneous clays, the nearest equivalent for the local potters was the opacification of their already existing transparent glazes with tin oxide. This made a thick white glaze to cover up the wares' coarse buff body. After glazing, the Islamic potters could not resist decorating the plain white surfaces which had been created – and so added their own strong and distinctive decorative idioms which could hardly be further removed from the restrained Chinese models. The colour palette was initially limited to using cobalt to give blue (the first known use of this pigment) and copper, giving blue-green.

A natural sensibility to the diverse qualities of brushwork is evident in the simple early designs – sometimes fine and graphic, sometimes bold and painterly – which also show a strong instinct for composition. Motifs were mostly stylised floral patterns, Kufic inscriptions or geometric devices.

Concurrent with the development of simple oxide decoration was the introduction of reduced-pigment lustres. These were developed from earlier use on glass, and were applied to the already fired tin glaze. Compounds of silver and copper were used to promote a variety of metallic lustre effects ranging from yellows, ambers and oranges to greens, browns and rich, coppery reds.

The spread and development of tin-glazed earthenware was inextricably linked to the rapid growth of Islam, extending throughout the Middle East,

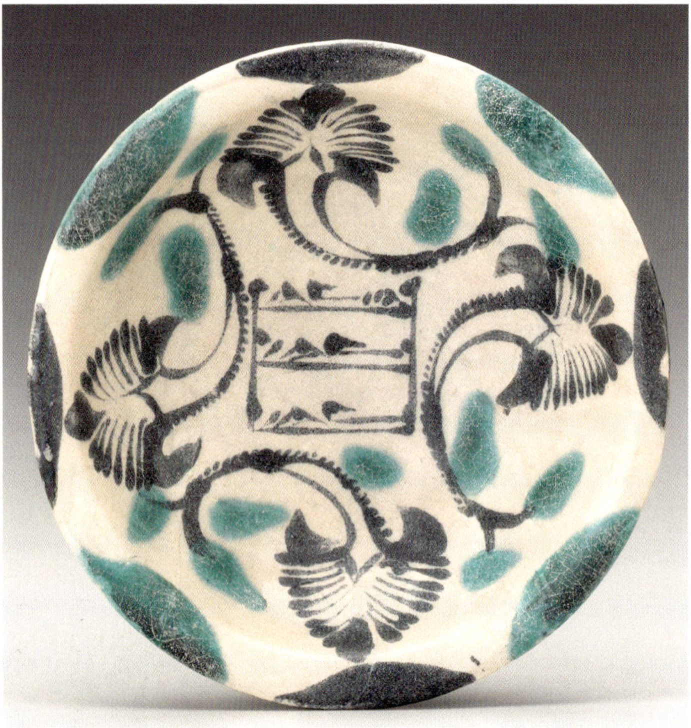

Bowl, Iraq, Abbasid period, 9th century. Dia: 21 cm (8 in.), ht: 5.7 cm (2¼ in.). *Freer Gallery of Art, Smithsonian Institution, Washington, D.C. Purchase, F2000.2.*

across North Africa and up into Moorish Spain. The 'Golden Age' of Spanish ceramics began in the mid-13th century with the production at Malaga of tin-glazed, lustred pottery, probably by potters who had come from Egypt. The fusion of Eastern and Western cultures brought a new vitality, nobility and flamboyance to the art of vessel-making, which was to become a paradigm for decorative earthenware throughout the whole of Europe. Some pottery centres, such as Paterna, produced simple, country-style pieces painted in manganese brown and copper green; others executed more elaborate designs using the *cuerda seca* technique (see p.66). The most impressive pieces, however – the albarellos, chargers and winged vases – were produced using cobalt blue in-glaze and metallic lustres on-glaze.

The Italian nobility held these wares in high esteem and began to commission commemorative and armorial pieces for themselves. These were exported to Tuscany in large quantities and became known in Italy as *maiolica* – most possibly after 'Majorca', which was an important port for trade at that time.

Tin-glazed earthenware as developed by the Italians is extraordinary in the history of ceramics for its elevation almost to the ranks of the fine arts. The tremendous potential for colour on tin-glazed ware was no doubt partly responsible for the high status it acquired.

The production of 'archaic' maiolica (sometimes also called Orvieto ware) in Italy was quite well established by the middle of the 13th century in Tuscany and Umbria. Some of the vessel forms

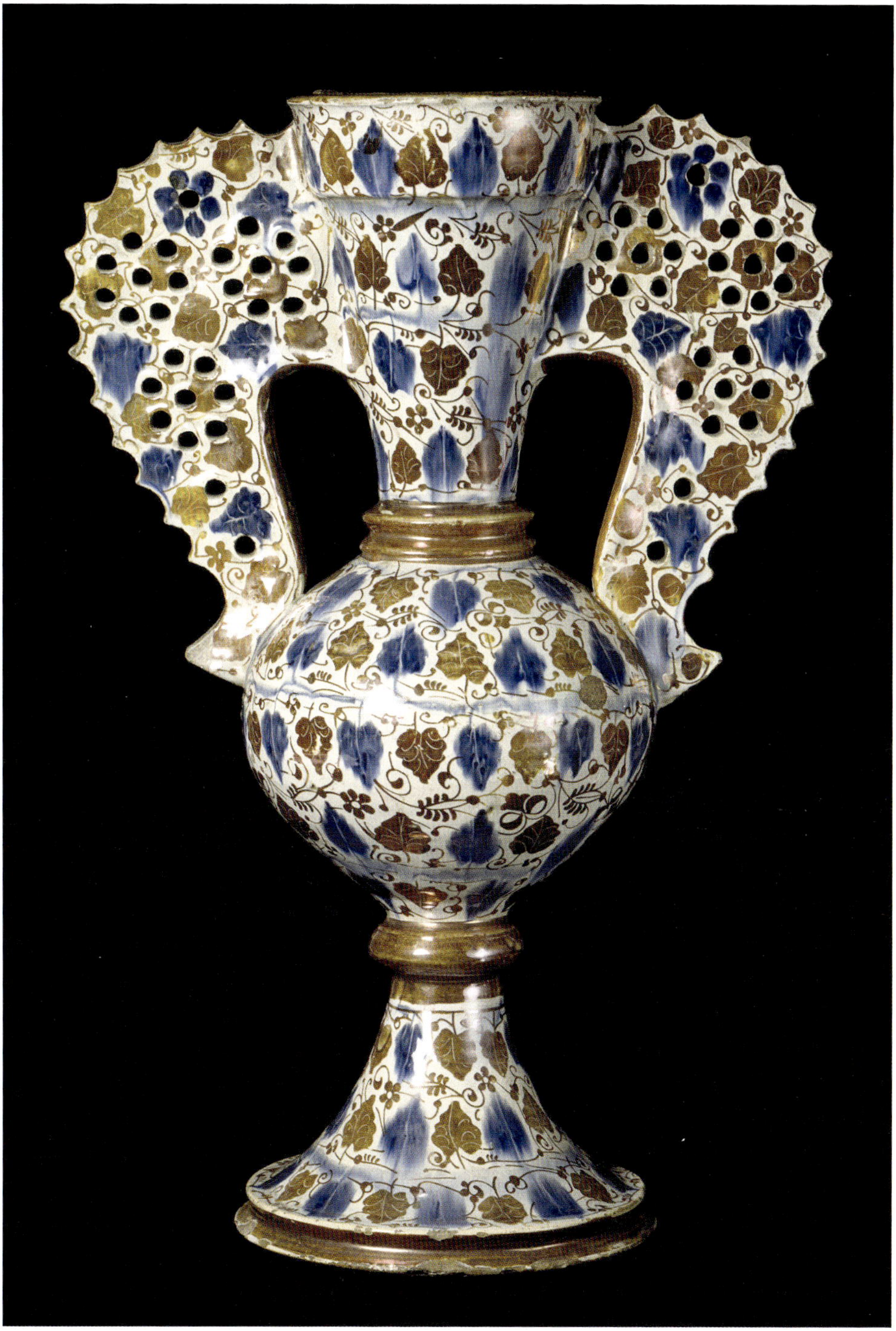

Winged vase, Valencia, 15th-century. Ht: 52 cm (20½ in.). *Photo © Victoria and Albert Museum, London.*

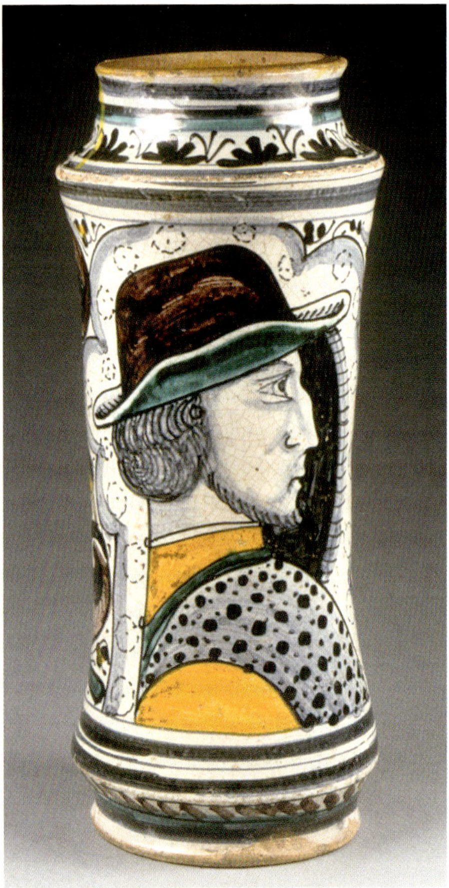

Albarello, Naples, late 15th century. Ht: 32.4 cm (12¾ in.). *Fletcher Fund. Metropolitan Museum of Art New York.*

referred back directly to the Islamic tradition, notably the albarello and other drug-jar shapes, but now distinctive new forms were also beginning to emerge. These were particularly evident in the jugs – pear-shaped pedestal jugs, jugs with thrown and applied lips, and loosely-shaped trilobate jugs. The simple painted designs, in copper green and manganese brown, are mostly geometric and articulate the forms.

Florence and Faenza were the two main centres for new developments in style and colour during the 1500s. Faenza saw the development of a repertoire of patterns in the vibrant, classic Italianate colour palette with various combinations of cobalt blue, copper green, manganese brown, lead-antimonate yellow and rusty orange (lead-antimonate with red iron). The use of this palette was to spread not only throughout Italy, but is also recognisable in early French faience and both Dutch and English Delftware.

In Florence, a range of distinctive wares was produced, including the relief-blue 'oak-leaf' drug jars and jugs with thick dark blue glaze over the tin white glaze and manganese outlines. These show strong influence from Hispano-Moresque designs.

By the mid-1500s, the powerful influence of Renaissance painting was obvious in the changing style of maiolica decoration, both in subject matter and manner of execution. The painted designs became increasingly sophisticated and usually depicted a narrative content. These wares are referred to as *istoriato*. The use of graded washes, fine lines and detail are evidence of the great skill of the decorators.

Alongside the painted wares, a new application of tin glaze was developed in the workshop of Luca della Robbia, a Florentine sculptor who had previously worked with marble, stone and bronze. Inspired by the colourful maiolica being produced by the potteries in Florence, he began to develop white and coloured tin glazes and applied them to his architectural reliefs and decorative roundels. This set a precedent for tin-glazed wares being embellished with modelled details, and also to the creation of more individual pieces that did not

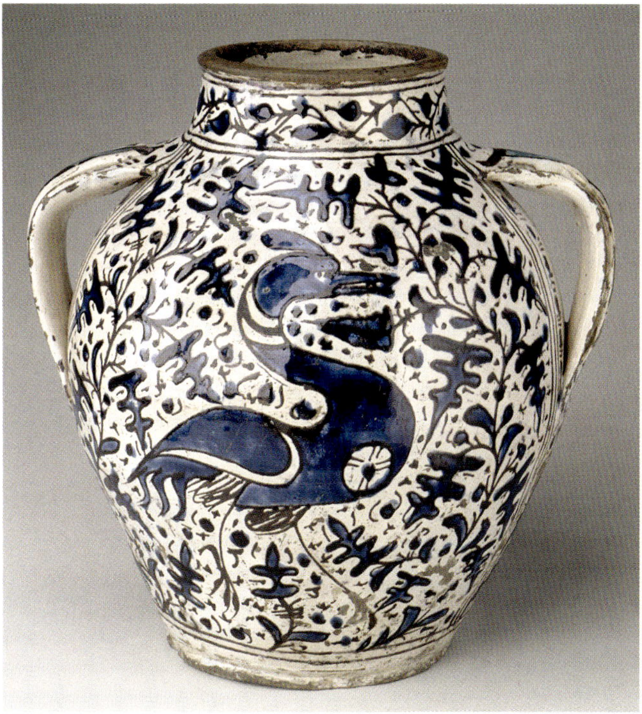

Apothecary jar, Florence, c. 1431. Ht: 31.5 cm (12½ in.). *Robert Lehman Collection, Metropolitan Museum of Art, New York.*

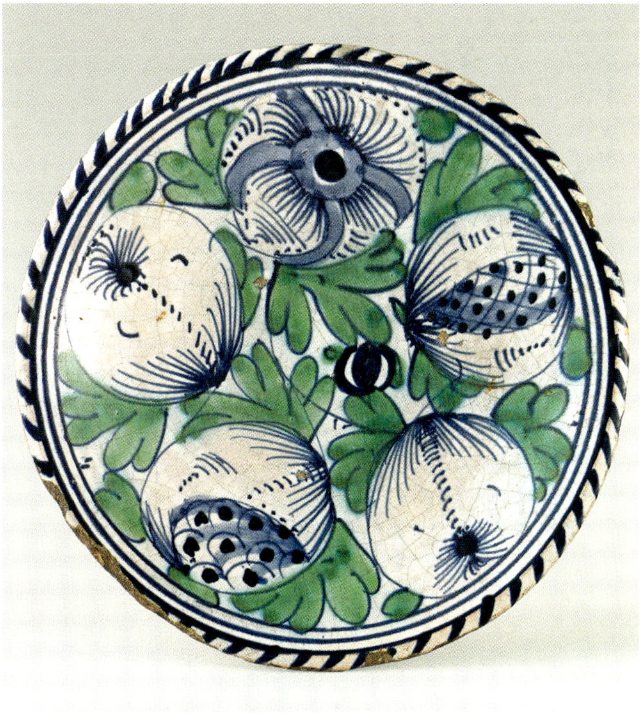

Charger with pomegranates, The Netherlands, 1610–1630. Dia: 25 cm (9¾ in.), ht: 4.5 cm (1¾ in.). *Photo: Musee Nationale de la Ceramique, Sevres.*

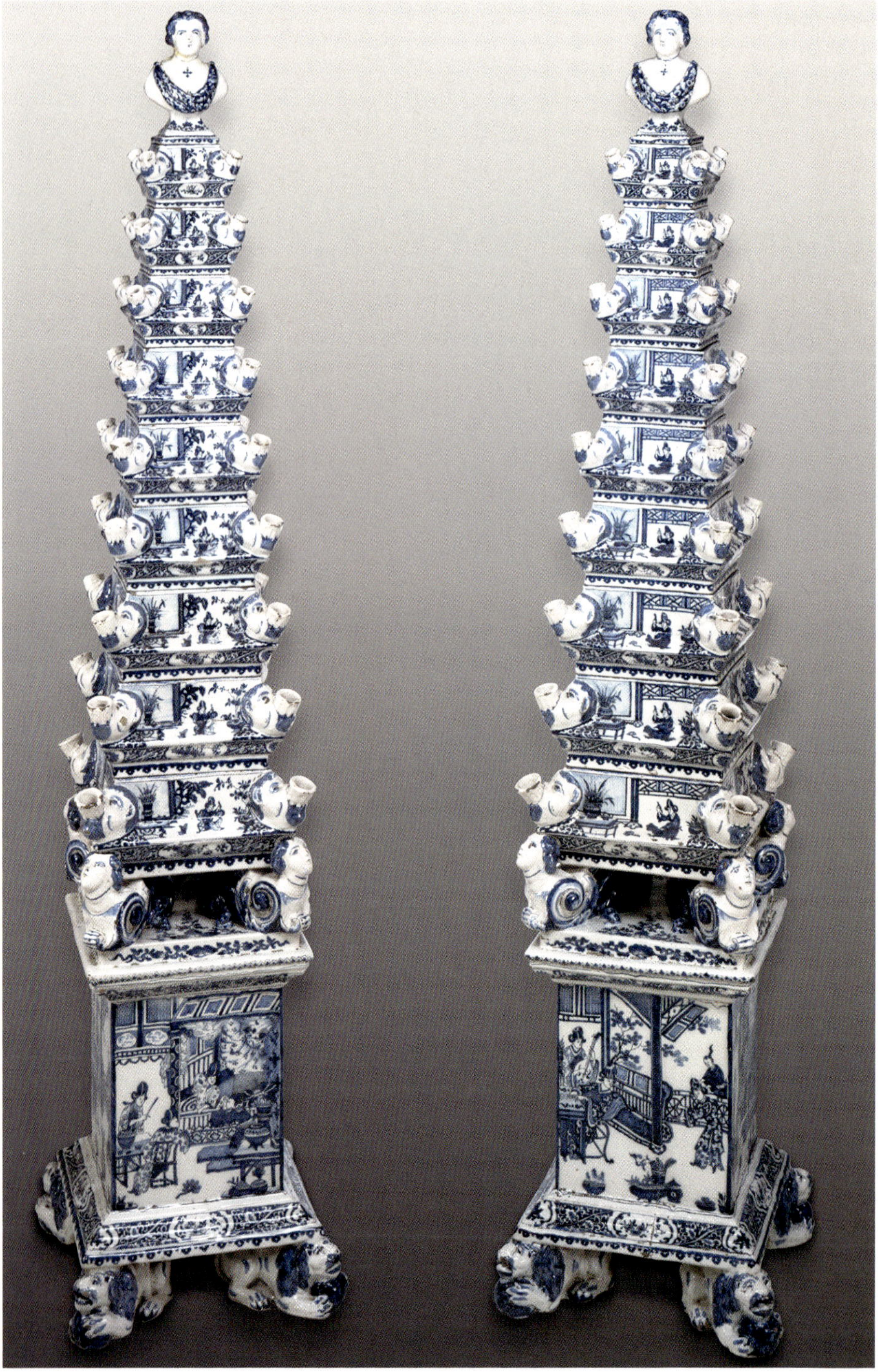

Flower pyramids, Delft, c. 1690, Ht: 160 cm (63 in.). *Photo © Victoria and Albert Museum, London.*

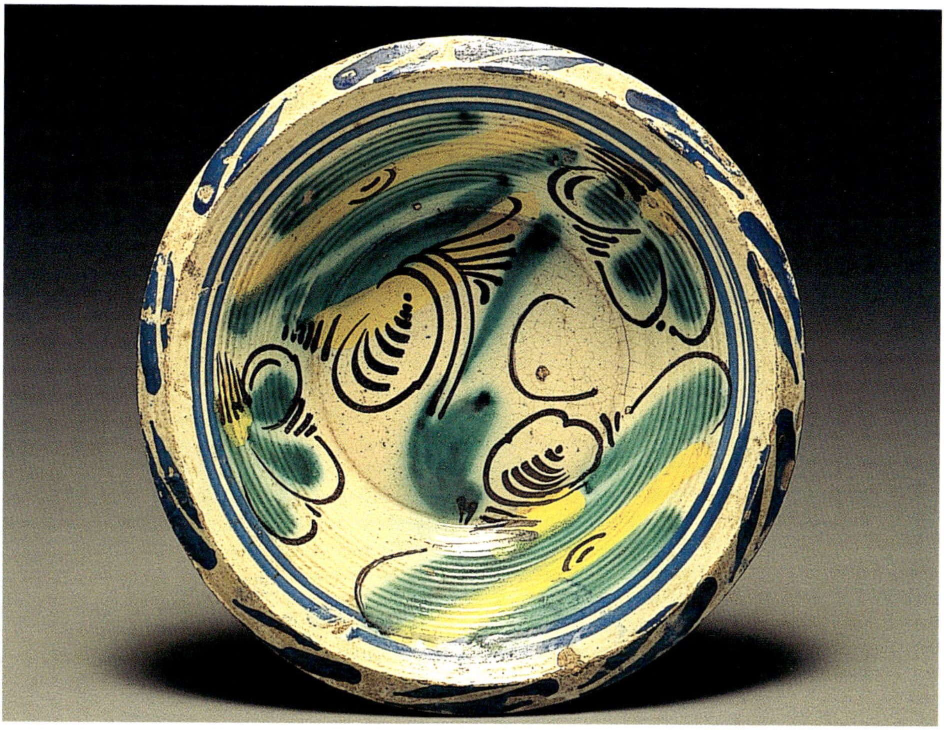

Dish, Triana, Spain, 19th-century. Dia: 30 cm (11¾ in.). *Collection of the author. Photo by Douglas Cape.*

necessarily have a utilitarian function. Maiolica used with relief or sculptural pieces has since become an integral part of the tin-glaze tradition.

The importance of maiolica as developed by the Italians cannot be underestimated, and Italy was to become the pivotal point from which tin-glazed earthenware with its new-found status in the decorative arts spread throughout Europe.

Most of the tin-glazed ware made in France in the 16th century closely resembled the Italian models – not surprisingly, as much was made by Frenchmen schooled by Italians. The main centres of production were Nevers, Rouen, Moustiers, Strasbourg and Marseilles, each with their own characteristics. Maiolica in France came to be known as 'faience', so called after the white tin-glazed wares of Faenza. Under the joint influences of Baroque art and Chinese porcelain, a new and distinctively French style emerged, but one which mainly still produced drug-jars.

17th-century faience, moving into architectural ceramics and tableware, is characterised by a cool, elegant classicism, mostly in a restrained blue and white palette – a reaction against the extravagant dynamics of the Baroque movement. The Rococo style dominates the 18th century, with extensive use of on-glaze enamels over tin glaze.

The Netherlands tin glaze industry also owed its inception to Italy, but its astonishing success to the porcelain of China. Tin-glazed earthenware here became known as 'Delftware', Delft being the main centre of its production.

Early Dutch and Flemish tin glaze is represented by the production of chargers, drug-jars and tile panels, still using the classic Italianate palette, but with distinctive, bold fruit and floral designs stimulated by a new interest in plants and horticulture.

The golden age of Delftware, the 17th and 18th centuries, was entirely driven by the desire to emulate Chinese Ming porcelain. Delft alone was able to develop both a superior body and glaze to gain the extra whiteness which this required. The use of a clear glaze (*coperta*) over the tin glaze gave an increased depth and luminosity to the intricate blue and white in-glaze painting.

Although tin-glazed ware in England started out, as in so many other countries, in the Italianate mode and emanated from Antwerp, it soon acquired a very different character from that of its European counterparts. In parallel with the qualities of the slipware made by Thomas Toft and his contemporaries, it typically exhibits a relaxed tone and a sprightliness which is preserved throughout the history of what was to become known as 'English Delftware'.

The overriding mood is provincial and naïve rather than urbane and sophisticated; in contrast to the highly fashion-conscious French faience and the impeccably high technical standards of Dutch Delftware, the English products remained on a much more humble level – their patronage consisting chiefly of middle-class merchant families and country gentry. The status of the potter was more lowly than that of his continental counterparts; the wares were less refined in both their intent and their execution. Typical examples include 'blue-dash' chargers with their recurrent and variable themes of Adam and Eve, floral designs and royal portraits, and also flower bricks, posset-pots and barbers' bowls.

Following the introduction by Wedgwood in the 18th century of white and cream earthenwares with their cheaper materials and methods of production, tin-glazed earthenware production on an industrial scale in Europe virtually died out. However, it continued both in the production of localised country potteries with a strong vernacular tradition, as at Quimper in France and Triana in Spain, and also as a medium of the individual artist.

Tin-glazed earthenware presented the perfect vehicle for painter exploration, and it has been closely linked to movements in the fine and applied arts – uncompromised by concerns of mass production and profitability. Artists who have made use of the particular qualities of tin glaze include Matisse, Vlaminck, Rouault, Redon and Renoir, who were all working in the Paris workshop of André Metthey in the early years of the 20th century. Roger Fry, founder of the London-based Omega Workshops, was so inspired by the faience of the French artists that tin-glazed earthenware became the medium of choice for Omega's production of ceramics. He saw the exhilarating, life-enhancing nature of bright colour and pattern as a corrective to the dinginess of the British home interior. Fry himself made many pots, which were often decorated by the artists Vanessa Bell and Duncan Grant.

London in the 1950s became the breeding ground for a new generation of maiolica potters – inspired by the ceramics of Picasso and a new Scandinavian design aesthetic. The

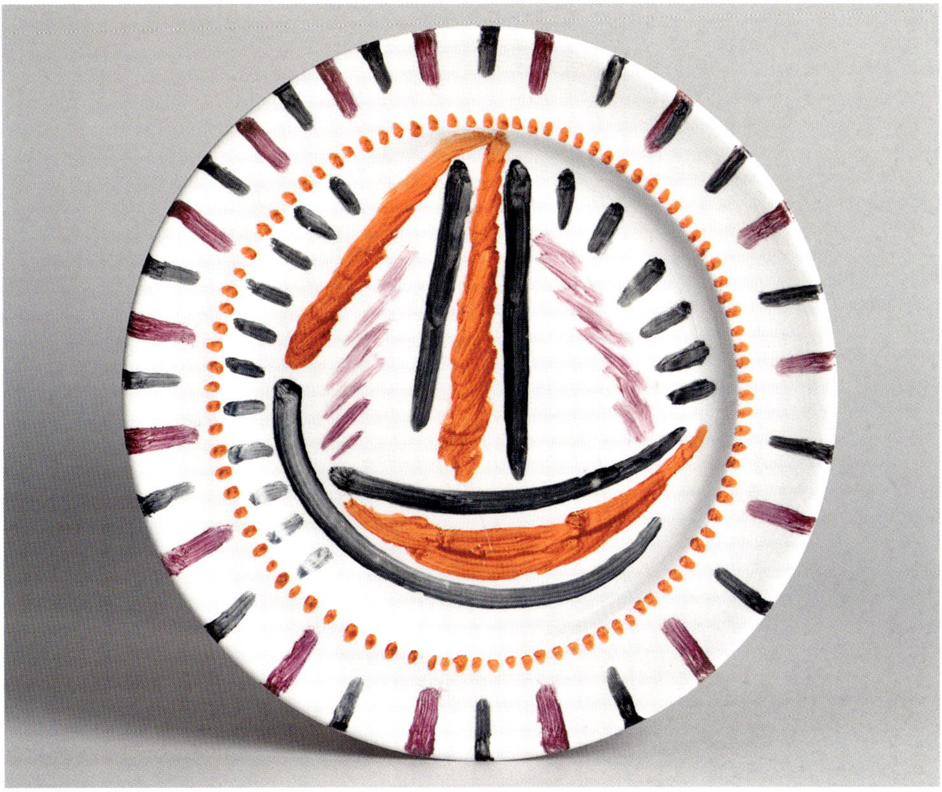

Omega Workshop (attributed to Duncan Grant), plate painted with a sailboat, 1913. Dia: 25 cm (10 in.). *Photo © Estate of Duncan Grant. All rights reserved, DACS 2010. Photo by Richard Valencia, courtesy of The Samuel Courtauld Trust, The Courtauld Gallery, London.*

practice of earthenware colour and decoration in ceramics was in strong contrast to the austere utilitarianism of the preceding war period, and also to the previously dominant oriental stoneware aesthetic which had been promoted by Bernard Leach.

Taught and encouraged by Dora Billington at the Central School of Art, William Newland, Margaret Hine, James Tower, Nicholas Vergette and Kenneth Clark were at the forefront of a revival of interest in maiolica – designing and making unique, hand-made pieces as well as architectural ceramics for the new coffee-bar culture. Apart from the likes of Newland, Kenneth and Ann Clark, Alan Caiger-Smith and Briglin Pottery, however, very little tin-glazed earthenware was produced from the late 1960s onwards. During this time, the main focus of ceramic interest swung firstly towards domestic stoneware, and then to the exploratory abstract vessels of ceramicists such as Alison Britton, Gordon Baldwin, Elizabeth Fritsch and contemporaries. By the 1980s, maiolica had made a comeback, and now takes its rightful place as a highly decorative and artistic medium.

Chapter 2

Basics: materials and procedures

Clay bodies

The main factors to consider when selecting a clay body for maiolica are:

- Colour
- Maturing temperature
- Function

The colour of the body can have a considerable effect on the colour of the glaze. A red earthenware body, for example, can lend a cooler, greyish hue to the fired glaze, whereas a white or buff body will produce a warmer, creamy white.

The maturing temperature of the body is particularly important if domestic maiolica is being made, as it has implications for crazing – undesirable and unhygienic for a porous body. To compress the glaze and so reduce crazing and porosity, bodies should be fired at the top end of their firing ranges. As a rule, a mature earthenware body, whether red or white, will always be preferable to an underfired stoneware body for functional ware. Maturity is not such an issue, however, for purely decorative or sculptural pieces.

Hand-built pieces, depending on their complexity, might require a more open body with greater strength and drying tolerance. This will make them less likely to crack or warp. A grogged red earthenware which is suitable for this purpose can either be bought ready prepared, or can be made up independently by adding an amount of fine or medium grog. Molochite can be added in a similar fashion to a white earthenware body.

Pieces made for permanent outdoor use, especially in cold winter climates, need to be frost-proof. This means firing to a high enough temperature to make the body vitreous or to give it minimal porosity – but without it becoming too brittle. Red clay on its own would therefore not be suitable, so experiments could be made with stoneware/red clay blends, fired to around 1180–1220°C (2156–2228°F). Maiolica effects are also possible at stoneware temperatures (see p.64).

Red earthenware bodies

These are probably the most popular choice as all-round, highly plastic and well-behaved clay bodies which mature within the range of most maiolica glazes. They are equally suitable for throwing or handbuilding. Most commercially available red earthenware bodies are strong, resistant to thermal shock, and have a wide firing range with maturity limits ranging from 1040°C to 1160°C (1904–2120°F).

Another obvious attraction is their warm terracotta colour,

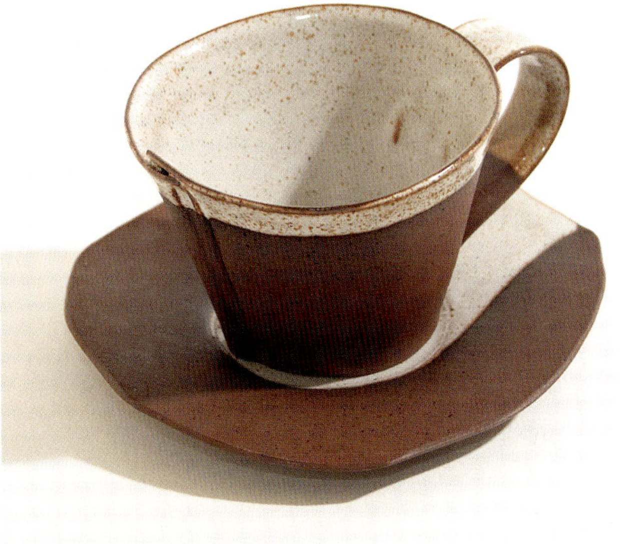

Cup and saucer by Jessica Wall. W (saucer): 16 cm (6¼ in.). Tin glaze on red earthenware body, fired to 1260°C (2300°F). *Photo by Laura King Photography.*

ranging from bright orangey-red at lower earthenware temperatures (1000–1060°C/1832–1940°F) to increasingly darker reddish brown at higher earthenware temperatures (1080–1140°C/1976–2084°F). The colour of the red body provides an excellent contrast to the milky white of the glaze. Some red earthenware bodies have a wider firing range, and can even withstand firing to 1200°C (2192°F) upwards.

The higher the glaze firing temperature, the greater the interaction between the body and the glaze. Higher temperatures also cause iron to be picked up from the body, creating a mottled glaze, which will 'break' on any edges and textures. This can be attractive, although it has a very different appearance from the solid white opacity of the traditional maiolica glaze. Jessica Wall is one practitioner who has exploited this quality for her hand-built tableware.

White earthenware bodies

It is the very whiteness of these commercially prepared bodies which is their main attraction, but this can sometimes be at the expense of plasticity and workability. There is no iron in the body to affect the colour of the glaze, and the result is a pure, warm white glaze. The whiteness of the body also means that you can get away with either a thinner coat of glaze or less opacifier.

The maturing range of these bodies tends to be higher than those of red earthenware bodies, and porosity and crazing can be a problem. Traditional industrial practice is to bisque-fire high to maturing temperature, and then glost-fire to a lower temperature. This way, the body is able to be supported in the bisque firing to avoid warping, and is left both non-porous and strong. The main problem with this procedure is that the body, being non-porous, does not readily absorb the glaze, and either the glaze has to be thickened (through flocculation) or the

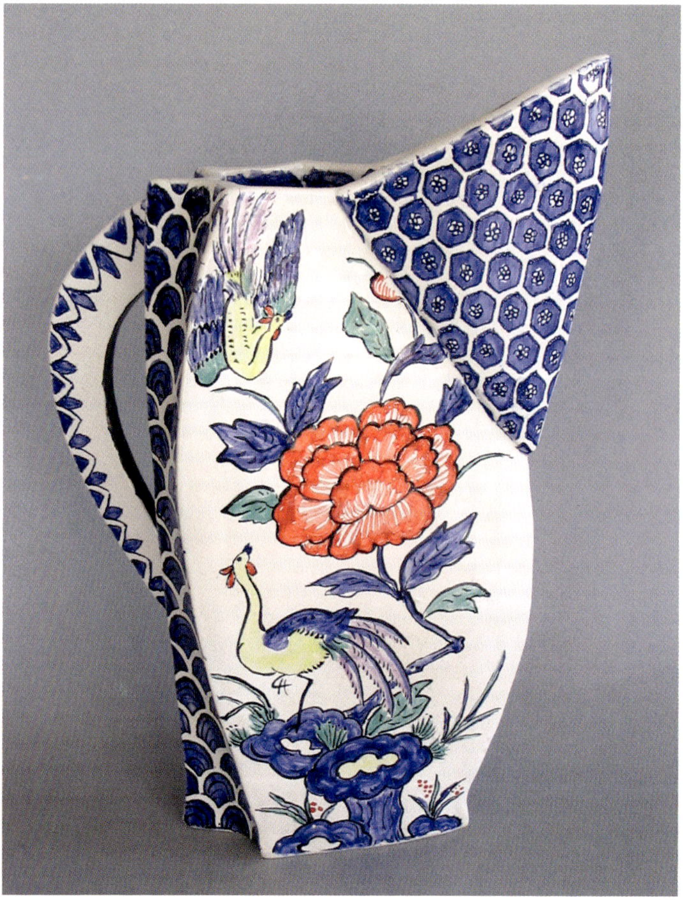

Jug by Gloria Young. Ht: 37.5 cm (14¾ in.). Slab-built using Potclays Studio White Earthenware, bisque-fired to cone 01, glost fired to cone 04. *Photo courtesy of the artist.*

body heated in order to achieve a suitable and even glaze thickness. The alternative is to fire to a standard biscuit temperature of 1000°C (1832°F), and then to fire up to maturity with the glaze firing. However, the range and quality of commercially available white earthenware bodies is now greatly improved, so it is worthwhile experimenting with a variety of bodies to find the best one for your purposes. Gloria Young uses a white earthenware body which is high bisque-fired and low glost fired.

Stoneware bodies

These are used by stoneware maiolica practitioners (see p.64), but are generally less suitable for use with low-fired maiolica, as they tend to mature at temperatures much higher than those of the standard maiolica glazes. However, they can be used for decorative and sculptural pieces or where porosity and crazing are otherwise unimportant, as they do provide a sympathetic pale base for the glaze. Amy Cook finds an ivory stoneware body eminently suitable for her finely decorated pieces.

Glaze composition

Maiolica glaze composition is based on industrially prepared frits – typically lead bisilicate frit, borax frit and alkaline frit.

These frits are often used in combinations so as to create a stable complex silicate. Frits represent the flux component of the glaze, which acts as a melting agent for the glass-forming silica content. Colour response, surface quality and opacity are all factors determined by the nature of the primary flux (lead, soda, potash or boric oxide), by any addition of the so-called secondary fluxes (e.g. whiting, zinc oxide, barium carbonate, talc, bone ash), and by the relative amount of alumina (usually introduced in the form of china clay) in the glaze. The glass-forming silica content is mostly provided by the frits and china or ball clay.

Fluxes are provided by the frits. The dominant flux will be the main factor in determining the surface quality, glaze colour and colour response of the in-glaze pigments.

Frits are made from fluxing oxides and silica, and can be thought of as powdered glass. They can be combined to create desired effects, for example, lead bisilicate may be combined with borax frit to reduce the yellowy hue given by the lead.

Lead frits (lead bisilicate, lead sesquisilicate)

The advantages of using lead frits in a maiolica glaze are:

- elasticity and low coefficient of expansion, thus minimising crazing
- bright, smooth surface with deep lustrous shine – stabilising, slow-maturing qualities with good smoothing-over after release of gases
- good colour response with most colouring oxides, notably rutile, iron, manganese, copper and cobalt

The disadvantages are:

- toxicity – under-fired lead glazes or those with too high a lead content can produce lead release, particularly when used in combination with copper oxide. This makes them dangerous; all lead-based glazes produced for domestic use should be tested for lead release (see p.108). US regulations on lead release are more

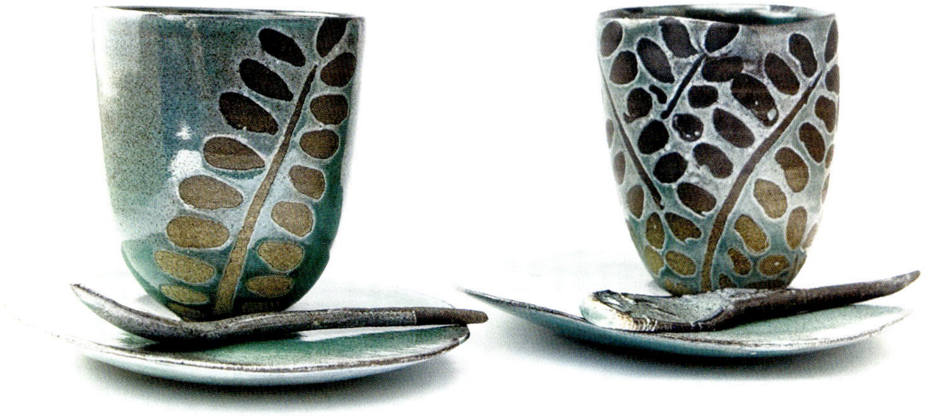

Fern Cups, Saucers and Spoons by Amy Cook. Ivory stoneware, black slip, wax resist and copper-coloured tin glaze. *Photo by Andrew Swarbrick.*

stringent than those applied in the UK, and most North American potters use lead-free glazes in reflection of this.
- High lead content can dissolve tin oxide and reduce opacity, thus necessitating a higher percentage of opacifier.
- Lead naturally has a yellowy colour, and this will modify the colour response accordingly – e.g. copper will become a more yellowy green than a bluey green.

Alkaline frits
These are made from varying combinations of soda and potash, often with some added boric oxide. Alkaline oxides have a high coefficient of expansion and are therefore prone to crazing, and they also tend to be unstable and lack fired strength. However, on the positive side, their natural milkiness creates a good starting point for opacification, and they promote a brilliant colour response – notably turquoise blue-green with copper and plum tones with manganese.

Borax frits
These are very useful either on their own or in combination with lead or alkaline frits. Boric oxide has a low coefficient of expansion and will therefore discourage crazing. It also helps to produce a balanced glaze, and will whiten a lead glaze and give a brighter colour response.

Calcium borate frit
Colemanite and gerstley borate (the latter no longer mined) appear in many American recipes. They are natural boro-calcite frits, and introduce boric oxide and calcium to a glaze. Gerstley borate also contains some sodium oxide. In the UK, it is advisable to substitute calcium borate frit for either of these materials; the form of colemanite available there is quite soluble and will cause the glaze to 'splutter' (mostly on to the kiln shelf!). Calcium borate frit is useful in small quantities as a balancing flux, encouraging opacity and helping to avoid crazing. Larger amounts will, however, tend to dull colours.

Zircon-borax frit
This is a borax frit which is already opacified with zirconium silicate, and is therefore a useful starting point for a maiolica glaze.

Feldspars, because of their high proportion of alumina and silica, cannot be used as a main fluxing material in earthenware glazes. However, they are often used in maiolica glazes because of their complex composition, which introduces alkaline fluxes of soda and potash as well as alumina and silica into the glaze. They also encourage opacification.

Secondary fluxes are less powerful than the primary fluxing frits mentioned above, but are often used to bring particular surface qualities to a glaze. 2–3% zinc oxide, for example, increases hardness, shine and opacity, and 8–10% will produce a pleasing, silky matt crystalline surface. It strongly intensifies cobalt blues, but can have a muddy effect on other colouring oxides – notably chrome. Up to 10% whiting (calcium carbonate) in a glaze will improve durability and reduce lead solubility. Larger amounts will promote opacity and produce a crystalline matt surface, but one which will tend to dull colours. Talc (magnesium silicate) and barium carbonate have good anticraze properties and will give matt opaque crystalline surfaces. Barium carbonate will also give heightened colour responses similar to those of the alkaline frits, but because of its toxicity should not be used for domestic glazes.

Opacification is favoured by certain conditions in a glaze; a greater amount of opacifier is required to opacify a glassy, transparent glaze, than one which is already viscous and/or crystalline. A greater amount is also necessary when using the glaze on a red earthenware body rather than on a white body. A glaze which is not rendered fully opaque by the addition of 10% tin oxide could readily be altered in composition to create a more receptive base for opacification by increasing the china clay or feldspar content. The degree of opacity is also dependent on the degree of fusion in the glaze. Although maiolica glazes are stable and have a wide firing range, they will be more matt and a denser white at the lower end of the range, and more lustrous and translucent at the top end. The main opacifying agents are tin oxide, zirconium silicate and titanium dioxide. These are often used in combination with one another.

Tin oxide creates opacity through its undissolved particles, which remain in suspension in the glaze. Traditional tin glazes often contained as much as 20% tin oxide. Such large amounts of tin increase the viscosity of the glaze; they can, however, cause pinholing, crawling and excessive mattness. 8–10% is a more typical addition today, if the glaze is well adjusted. For many maiolica practitioners, tin gives an unrivalled quality of opacity with its soft, milky whiteness. The only drawback is its facility for attracting chrome. Any form

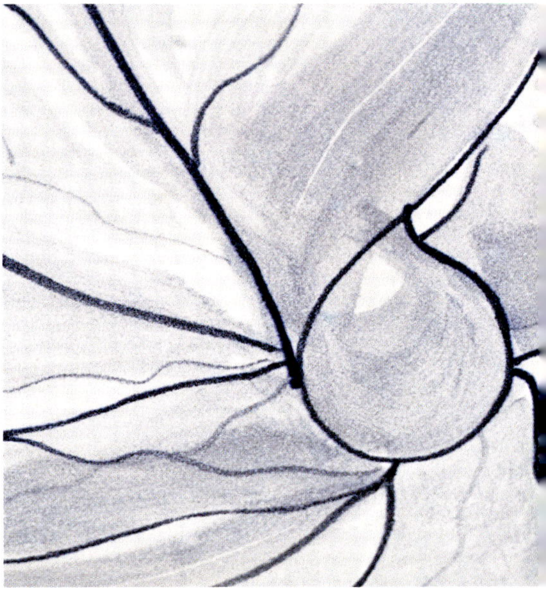

Agave dish by Daphne Carnegy, 2009. Detail showing painting in black stain on milky white pure tin-opacified glaze. *Photo by Sussie Ahlburg.*

of chromium oxide in the kiln will migrate and form pink flashes on the glaze surface, particularly where calcium is present in the glaze. Chrome-tin pink stains make positive use of this property, whereas many industrially prepared stains which contain chrome will create an unpleasant yellow colouration around the stain. Tin oxide is also expensive.

Zirconium silicate is very commonly used as an opacifier, either on its own or in combination with tin oxide. A big advantage of using this opacifier is that it costs about one-quarter of the price of tin oxide. However, greater quantities are needed to gain a similar opacity; if 10% tin oxide gives a good opacity, then up to 15% zirconium silicate will be needed to create a similar effect. Very fine grades of zirconium silicate are available – Zircosil 5

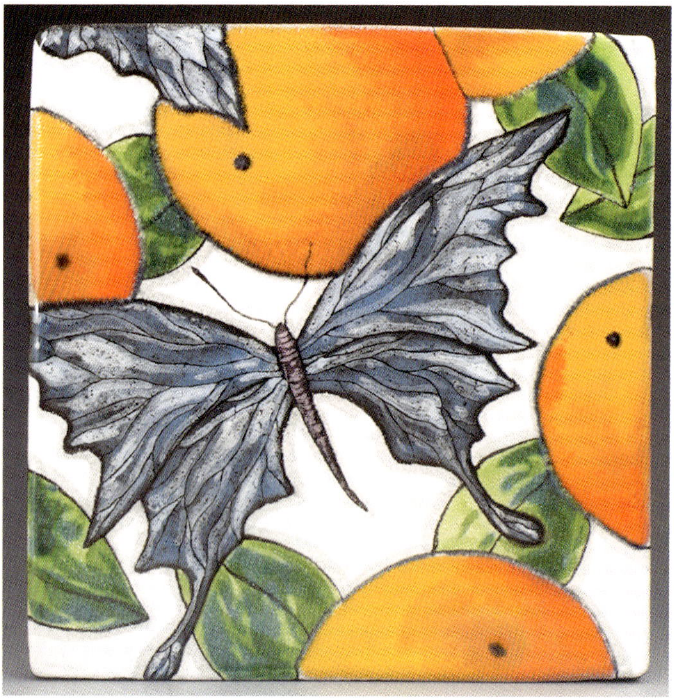

Oranges and Blue Morpho Butterflies by Farraday Newsome, tile, 2009. 20 × 20 × 0.5 cm (8 × 8 × ¼ in.). The glaze is based on Ferro frit 3124, with 20% Zircopax for extra whiteness. *Photo courtesy of the artist.*

in the UK and Zircopax or Superpax in the USA. In comparison with tin, some consider the quality of whiteness imparted by zircon to be harsher, and the sensitivity of colour response less acute. Small additions of rutile (0.5 to 1%) can be added to soften the whiteness. The material is redeemed by its tolerance of chrome, however, and is therefore particularly suitable for those working mostly with commercial stains.

Titanium dioxide, in combination with other opacifiers, will give a creamy tone and a rich satin surface when used in small amounts. The colour response which it gives is toned down by its creaminess so that cobalt oxide, for example, will become more greeny in tone. However, this more subdued palette can be very attractive, and titanium will also enhance any iron bearing pigments such as red iron oxide, rutile and ilmenite.

Glazing

The process of glazing is (still!) for me, and I suspect for others, a bit of a nerve-racking procedure. Despite my best efforts, I am never totally sure of the thickness of application, and am always greatly relieved once the first glaze firing is successfully out of the way. A calm, methodical approach and plenty of space are the best prerequisites for trouble-free glazing.

Preparation of the glaze

The glaze should be mixed up at least 24 hours before use. After weighing the dry ingredients, they need to be thoroughly mixed prior to adding them to the water. Use plenty of water to facilitate sieving, as the water content will be adjusted once the glaze has settled. Stir well to mix, and then sieve twice – once through 60s or 80s mesh, and once through 100s or 120s mesh. The glaze should then be left to settle; it will have been temporarily flocculated by the mixing activity, and although it may appear thick enough to use, this appearance will usually be deceptive. When the glaze has settled, you can skim off excess water and so test the glaze thickness more accurately; getting to know the right thickness for your particular glaze takes time and experience, but generally speaking, the residue left on a dipped hand will give a good indication. You can also test by scratching through the dried surface of a dipped test piece – a fairly standard thickness is 1–2 mm. Cipriano Piccolpasso, writing at the time of the Italian Renaissance in his *The Three Books of the Potter's Art*, describes this same method and concludes that the ideal thickness is that of 'the edge of one of those skins used for making gloves'!

Maiolica glazes which contain a large proportion of non-clay materials such as frits tend to settle quite rapidly. To combat this, the addition of 2% bentonite will help to keep the glaze in better suspension. However, it is essential that the bentonite is well integrated into the dry mix before any water is added, as it is almost impossible to add into a liquid glaze due to its fine particles and super-plasticity. If settling is still a problem and there is some clay content in the glaze (e.g. china clay or ball clay), a flocculant such as epsom salts or calcium chloride (½ to 3 tablespoons to 20 litres of glaze) can be added to give the glaze more bulk, increase adhesion and further reduce settling. The flocculant should be added progressively until the desired consistency is obtained. In low-clay

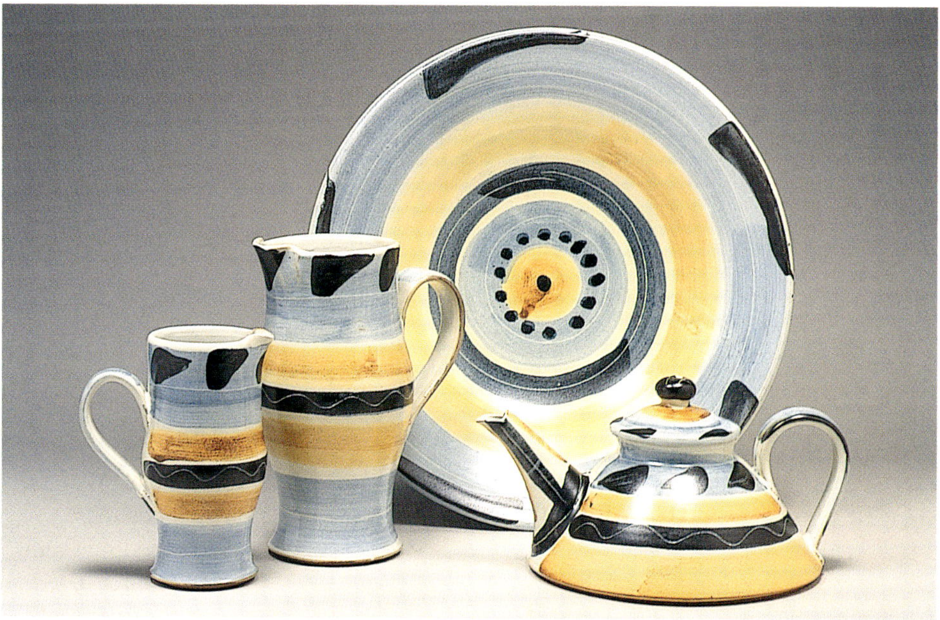

St Ives range by Daphne Carnegy, 2000. Oxide mixtures (no. 2, 5 and 17 on chart, see pp.34–5) on tin and titanium glaze (LB5). *Photo by Stephen Brayne.*

glazes, sodium carboxymethylcellulose (SCMC) can be used as a glaze binder to increase hardness, adhesion and viscosity (try 2%). For brushing on the glaze, sodium silicate will assist brushability.

Preparation of biscuit ware for glazing

It is worthwhile taking the trouble to prepare a good, blemish-free surface for glazing and painting. After biscuit firing, any rough bits and bottoms of pots can be sanded down with medium-grade wet and dry paper. In order to keep the glaze off bases and feet, these are all waxed (on the wheel for thrown pieces) with an old brush using hot candle wax which has been thinly diluted with paraffin – kept to the correct temperature in a bowl supported over a 60 watt light bulb.

Wax emulsion can also be used if preferred, although I find that it is not so readily absorbed by the biscuitware. Scraping and sponging of bases and feet after glazing is another option, particularly for one-off pieces. This method has the advantage of leaving a very fine, watery glaze film on the body which helps to seal it, without it being thick enough to stick to the kiln shelf. Prior to glazing, all biscuit-fired pots are wiped over with a damp sponge to remove the sanding dust and help absorption of the glaze into all the tiny air pockets in the porous biscuit. Otherwise, these air pockets could cause pinholes to occur in the glaze – particularly applicable to areas which have been turned and so had their grog brought to the surface. As an additional measure, after turning, it helps to compress the grainy surface with a kidney.

Applying the glaze

Dipping is the method of choice for maiolica glaze application. Make sure you mix up enough glaze to enable easy dipping – I usually make sure to have at least 15 kilos of glaze in a large bucket, topping it up as required. I also have a variety of different shaped containers so that larger, wider, taller pieces can be more easily dipped. These include cat-litter trays and baby baths!

It is preferable to glaze pots as quickly and evenly as possible, ideally dipping the whole piece in one go. This will minimise overlaps and runs. For large or awkward-shaped pieces, it is a good idea to 'rehearse' the process first (in the air). I use glazing tongs for most items, but if, for example, a large platter is a bit tight in the container and will not leave enough room for the tongs, two fingers on each hand, placed firmly on the rim, will suffice. The less touching up there is to do, the better.

Most of my pieces are designed with the glazing in mind so that, for example, my large bowls and dishes have a substantial waisted footring which can be held by the left hand as the piece is brought out of the glaze, with the tongs held in the right hand. For tall pieces, such as vases, I find it easier to glaze by rotating them on their sides in a baby bath, using tongs in the right hand and fingers under the base as support when bringing them out from the glaze slop. The pieces should be brought out of the glaze cleanly, and in the direction you wish the glaze to drain off, for example upside down for mugs and jugs, and on their sides for plates and bowls. It is better not to shake the freshly glazed pieces, as this may create more dribbles, but a finger is usually sufficient to catch any drips which do occur.

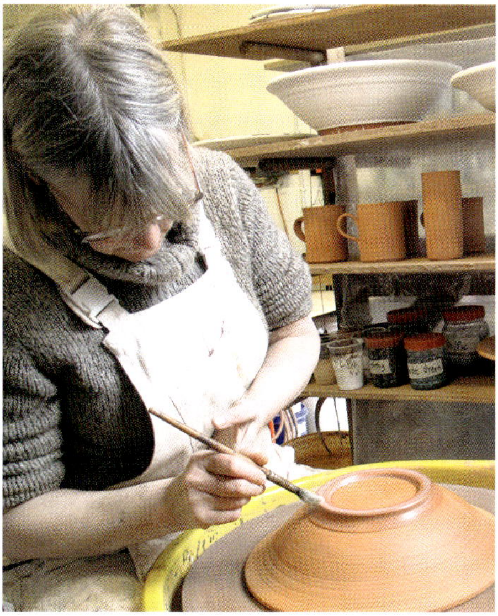

Waxing feet prior to glazing. The wax is kept hot over a light bulb. *Photo by Gunizi Amirak.*

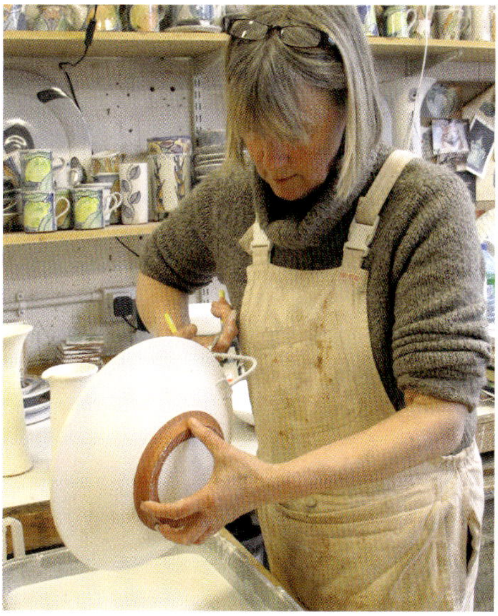

Glazing using tongs. *Photo by Gunizi Amirak.*

When I have a whole batch of pots to glaze, I start with the smaller items and work up to the larger ones; the smaller pieces are less absorbent due to the relative thinness of their walls, and so the glaze needs to be applied more thickly. I then add progressive amounts of water as I proceed on to glazing the larger pieces. Even with bentonite in the glaze, the glaze settles quickly – particularly in a large, wide container. I advise thorough stirring of the glaze at regular intervals during the glazing session. With larger pieces, this should be carried out in between the glazing of each piece.

Other methods of glazing are pouring (but beware of overlaps) and spraying, although the aerated surface is not ideal for painting on. Glazes vary in their raw surface qualities – the glaze I usually use (LB4, see p.100) luckily has a good hard but absorbent surface, helped by the presence of bentonite. If your glaze naturally has a very powdery raw surface, you could try adding either liquid laundry starch or SCMC as mentioned above.

Any touching up or fettling of the glaze should be done when the glaze has dried, and I do this just before decorating. Obviously finger marks need to be touched up – blobbing, rather than painting, on the glaze using a soft brush. Subsequent fettling will be required here. Tong scars will need just a cursory rub with a finger. On the whole, however, the glaze is best left undisturbed as far as this is possible, particularly on the surfaces which will be painted; fettling creates a powdery surface which can impede the flow of subsequent brushwork. On the other hand, maiolica glazes are not very forgiving, and any dribbles or overlaps of glaze will stay very visible under any colour work – less of a problem if your style is gestural and free, but more of a problem if you work in a graphic, detailed manner.

I like to leave glazed pieces for at least

24 hours before starting to decorate. A surface which is still damp will not be hardened, pigments will therefore not be well absorbed and brushwork will tend to pull off the glaze. Glazed pots can be left for as long as you like before decorating, but it is advisable to cover them to protect from dust.

Pigments: colouring oxides and stains

The following are some general observations and pointers on colour in maiolica. In-glaze colour on maiolica glazes is produced by the use of colouring oxides, commercial stains or underglaze colours. Their preparation and application are a continuous learning curve! With the colouring oxides, it takes considerable experience to get to know their strengths and weaknesses, and also to become familiar with the change of colour and tonal values which happens in the firing of many oxides – copper, for example, which looks black on application, can fire to a light green. It is important to learn to exploit the potential of each pigment – **cobalt** is strong and stable, and so suitable for fine details as well as broad brushwork, and is also highly responsive in varying strengths; **copper** is more volatile with a soft fused effect, unsuitable for fine lines but effective on larger areas; **iron** mixtures have a granular effect, etc.

Different surface textures will also be created according to how refractory or fluxing the pigments are – rutile mixtures, for instance, have to be used with care as they can become rough and blistered if too thick, but appropriately applied can create a lustrous, satin film which is pleasing to the touch. With the stains and underglaze colours, what you see is pretty much what you get – but here again, the preparation of the mixture and the thickness of application needs to be well judged in order to avoid rough, pitted surfaces.

The colouring oxides (typically cobalt, copper, manganese, iron and rutile) provide blues, greens, browns, ochres and blacks, whereas the stains and underglazes are useful for creating a wider range of colours which would be difficult to manufacture in a studio setting – for example, yellows, oranges, reds, purples etc. The two can complement each other quite well: the oxides subtle and variable in intensity, the stains stable and predictable (but on their own sometimes crude and bland, although I realise this is a matter of opinion!). The colouring oxides and stains can also be intermixed for a more individual palette, and endless combinations are possible. Choice of a colour palette is very personal, and it is worthwhile experimenting with a wide variety of combinations until you are satisfied. Colour theories that apply to painting are also relevant to ceramic colours, so if you have knowledge of these, it's worth putting it to good use, bearing in mind that the latter are not always so predictable.

Reference to a colour wheel shows which colours harmonise and which colours complement each other. Warm oranges and reds are complemented by cooler blues and violets, for example, whereas relatively pale colours such as yellows and oranges may need to be defined by the presence of stronger colours such as blues or blacks, as without these, they can look visually weak on the white background. Having

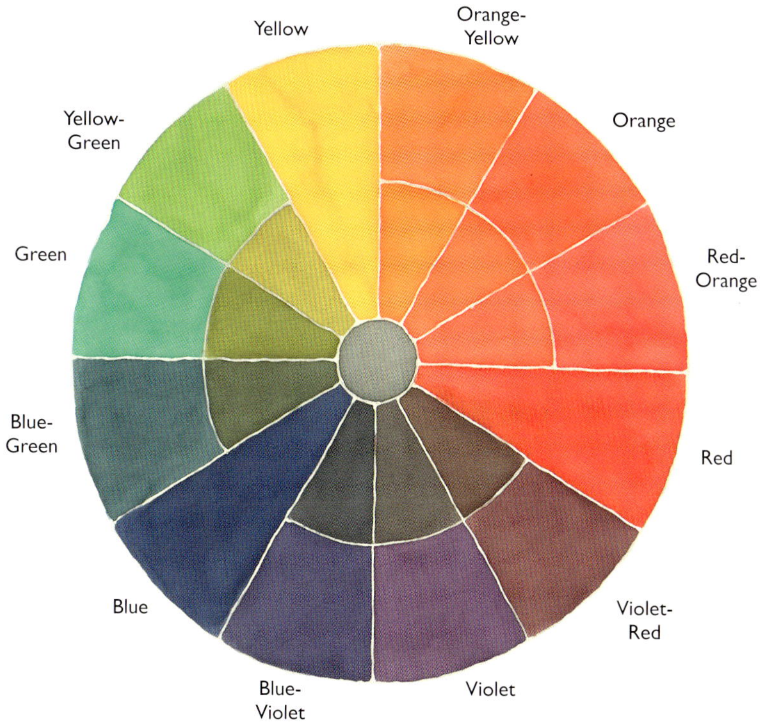

A basic colour wheel using primary and secondary colours painted on silk by Jane de Sausmarez. Photo © Jane de Sausmarez, from her book Basic Colour: A Practical Handbook..

said this, use of colour is of course subjective and will depened on the effect you want to achieve. The colour wheel can also be used as a guide to which pigments can be intermixed to create new colours – a yellow and a green can be mixed to give lime-green, etc.

The classic Italianate palette, so characteristic of Italian Renaissance maiolica and developed in Faenza in the late 15th century, formed a highly effective and complementary grouping of colours. Most dominant was a strong cobalt blue, used for lines, outlines and shaded backgrounds, offset by a soft turquoise copper green, a soft manganese purple-brown, a yellow (lead antimonate) and a rusty orange (lead antimonite and iron oxide). The tile-making company Reptile (comprised of Carlo Briscoe and Edward Dunn) work with a similar range of complementary and harmonising pigments – using mostly colouring oxides of cobalt, copper, manganese, iron and nickel with the added use of stains for red and yellow (see overleaf).

Tone and intensity of colour will affect the whole mood of the design – giving anything from pale, watercolour tones to vibrant, intense, saturated colours. Ceramic colours, however, are not as straightforward as artists' colours, and as already mentioned, what you see is not always what you get. The amount of water mixed with a pigment will largely determine its final intensity, but a great deal of experimentation is required to become familiar with the behaviour of the colouring oxides and stains.

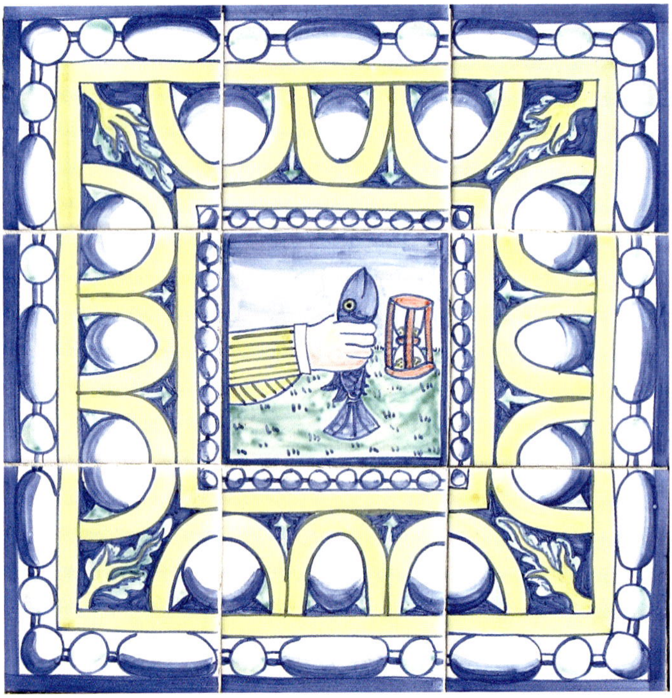

Fish In Hand tile panel by Reptile, each tile: 10 x 10 cm (4 x 4 in.). Painted in cobalt oxide, Naples Yellow and green (copper oxide 8, nickel oxide 1, by weight). *Photo courtesy of the artist.*

Colour palettes also evolve and change with time. I, for example, used to work with a spectrum of strong, vivid colours. Although I do still work with some of these colours, I have also discovered the delights of working with a much more limited palette – often just shades of blue or black, relying on tonal values rather than brilliant colours for effect. I also find that, having worked for a while with this more restrained palette, I tend to approach my polychrome work in a more economical and simple way, working with the pigments as I would with watercolours.

Colouring oxides – characteristics and uses

Cobalt oxide or carbonate

Gives blue. The most powerful oxide and also a strong flux. In the raw state it is black, unlike the slightly weaker cobalt carbonate which has the advantage of being a distinctive pink colour and therefore easily identifiable. A very stable oxide, the fired colour is much brighter and cruder than the impure oxide of historical tin-glazed earthenware. It is, however, easily toned down with one of the modifying oxides such as iron, manganese or nickel, or a little red clay. Cobalt is the most susceptible of the colouring oxides to 'breaking up' and texturing on a maiolica glaze. If used too thickly, it will become black and rough. Excellent for monochrome work, as different cobalt/water strengths work beautifully together. Being very stable, it is also a good colour for fine lines and detail. Can be used on its own, with water, mixed 1:1 by volume with china clay, or 1:1 with alkaline frit for heightened colour. (See also photo on p.101.)

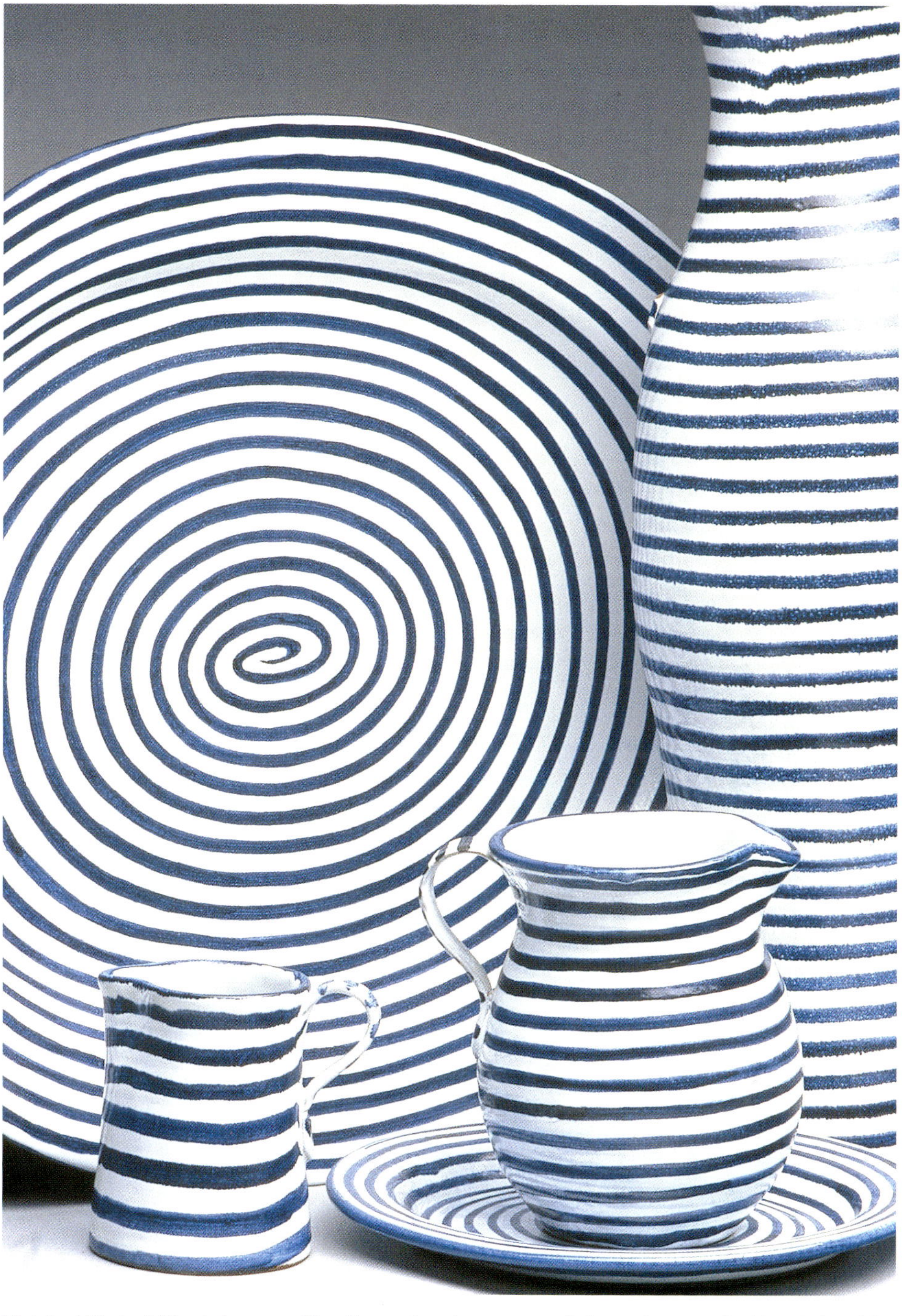

Majolica Works (Wendy Jones and Ian Ramsay) make a range of pieces decorated with cobalt oxide on tin glaze. Ht (tall jug): 56 cm (22¼ in.). The clay body is Valentines V636 terracotta, biscuit fired to 1010°C (1850°F). Glaze firing is 1115°C (2039°F) with 15 minute soak. *Photo by Joel Chester Fildes.*

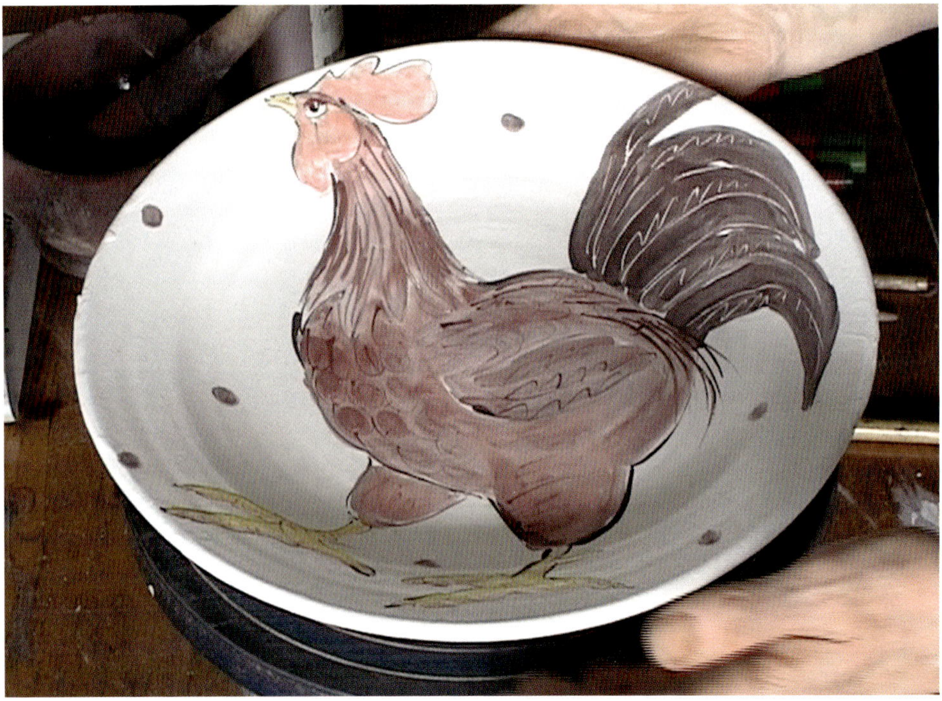

Copper oxide or carbonate
A strong flux, which in maiolica tends to give turquoise-greens, or even bluer results in alkaline glazes. It has a very soft, fuzzy quality, so is not good for precision painting, and is better as a filler or for broad brushstrokes. The oxide is black in the raw state, whereas the carbonate is green. I use the oxide in preference, as the carbonate is not so easily assimilated in water. This is also a strong oxide and will readily go metallic in appearance if applied thickly. It should not be used with lead-based glazes on tableware, as it promotes lead release in the presence of acidic substances such as fruit juices or vinaigrettes etc.

Manganese dioxide or carbonate
Produces cool browns to brown-black on lead-based glazes, pinkish to plum purple-browns on lead-free glazes. It works well as a foil for cobalt blues, and was much used in that combination in English Delftware. It is a relatively weak oxide, and has a pronounced speckle. It will go metallic black if applied thickly.

Red iron oxide
Rust colour in the raw state, it produces a grainy reddish-brown on maiolica glazes. It is a relatively weak colourant. The presence of zinc or zirconium in the glaze can dull the colour response, giving more murky browns. Titanium, however, works well with iron, and will yield warm yellow-orangey rust colours.

Nickel oxide
Gives an unusual khaki green. It is an excellent modifier of cobalt and copper, but is extremely refractory – used on its own, it requires the addition of frit to avoid a rough surface quality.

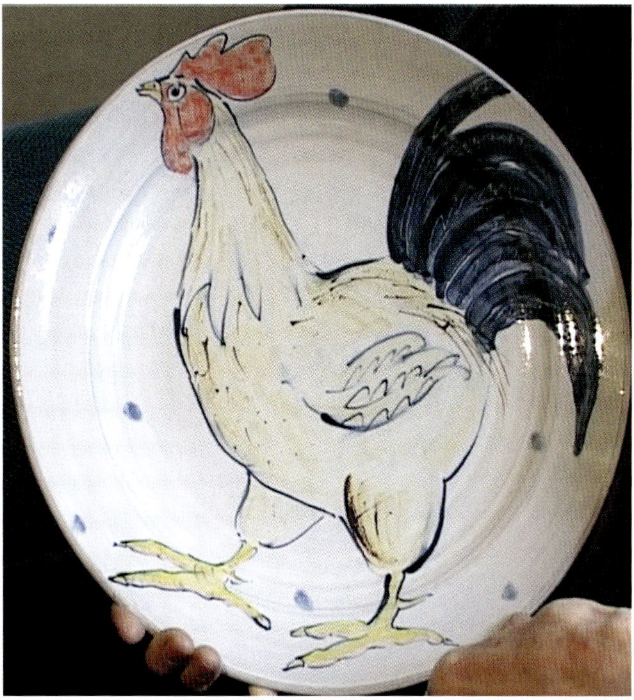

FAR LEFT *Cockerel* plate by Molly Attrill, before firing. The main body of the cockerel is painted in red iron oxide. *Photo by Shingy Mupesa, courtesy of Seagull Production.*

LEFT *Cockerel* plate by Molly Attrill, after firing. The change in tonal value of the red iron oxide from raw to fired is marked. *Photo by Shingy Mupesa, courtesy of Seagull Production.*

Rutile

This is an impure form of titanium dioxide with traces of iron, and on its own produces a slightly grainy ochre colour. It is highly refractory, and so is best fluxed with lead bisilicate. It is an interesting modifier of other oxides such as cobalt, copper and iron.

Ilmenite

Behaves a bit like a coarser form of rutile with a variable, higher iron content. Used unsieved, it can provide a grainy texture.

Chromium oxide

Rarely used on its own, as not only is it highly refractory, but it produces a rather flat 'park bench' green. Makes a useful component, along with iron and cobalt, of a compound black pigment. On a tin-opacified glaze it can be volatile, creating an unpleasant yellow staining on the surrounding glaze. The presence of zinc will turn chrome brown, and pinks and reds will be produced in the presence of both tin and calcium. Chrome is extensively used in the preparation of stains and underglaze colours, but if these commercial colours are regularly used, the underlying glaze should be zirconium-opacified.

Soluble colourants

Different qualities can be obtained by the use of soluble colourants such as copper sulphate (turquoise), cobalt sulphate (blue), iron sulphate (tan), manganese chloride (plummy brown) and chrome chloride (green). These are dissolved rather than suspended in water, so they suffuse the glaze to make very uniform, ground colours with a soft edge. Areas to be left white must be waxed before applying soluble colourants. (*Information courtesy of Linda Arbuckle*).

Stains and underglaze colours

Any commercial stains or underglazes (despite their name) can also be used as in-glaze pigments. The powdered form is best for standard preparation with frit or glaze.

Amaco produce a range of liquid velvet underglazes, only some of which work for in-glaze decoration – the others being too refractory. These need to be tested for suitability.

Amaco also produce a new range of colours specifically designed for maiolica in-glaze decoration – the Gloss Decorating Colours (GDCs). These are now quite widely used in the USA and Canada, and can be painted straight from the bottle on to the glaze.

Preparation of pigments

Pigments can be prepared in a great variety of ways, but the manner in which this is done depends to some extent on how they are going to be used and ultimately it is a matter of personal preference.

If you want the option of dry-blending after painting for a pastel effect, then mixing the pigments with frit or glaze and water is fine, as they remain powdery on the surface of the glaze. Oxides mixed with frit and water tend to settle quickly, however, and therefore need to be well stirred before each dip of the brush. If, on the other hand, a hard pigment surface is required – for example if you will be covering it with wax resist – then the addition of a little bentonite (well mixed with the dry pigment first) is recommended. The US ceramicist Linda Arbuckle finds that this method also improves the ease of the brushstroke.

Her general guidelines for preparing the oxides are as follows:

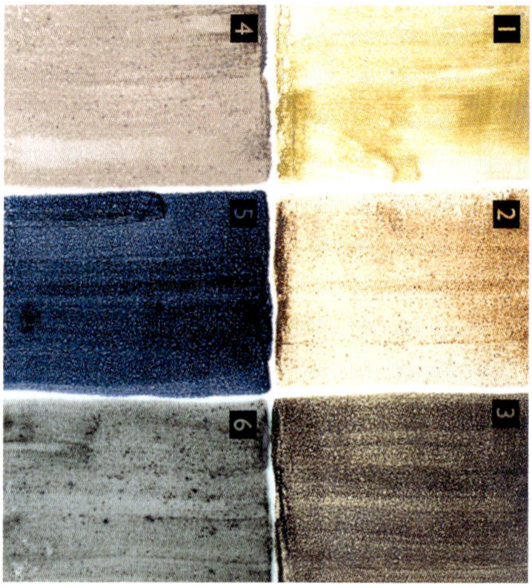

Oxide mixtures 1–6

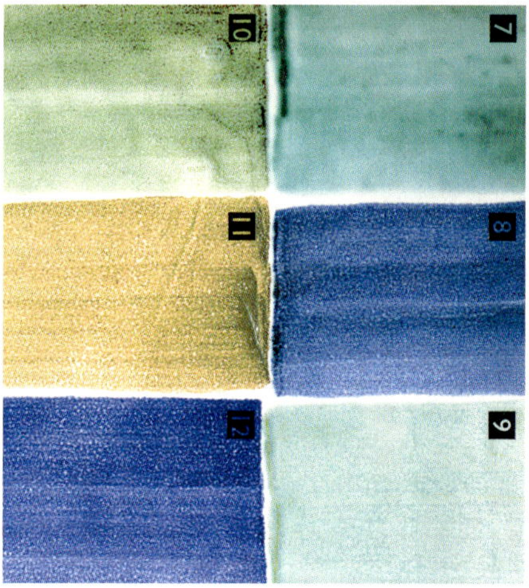

Oxide mixtures 7–12

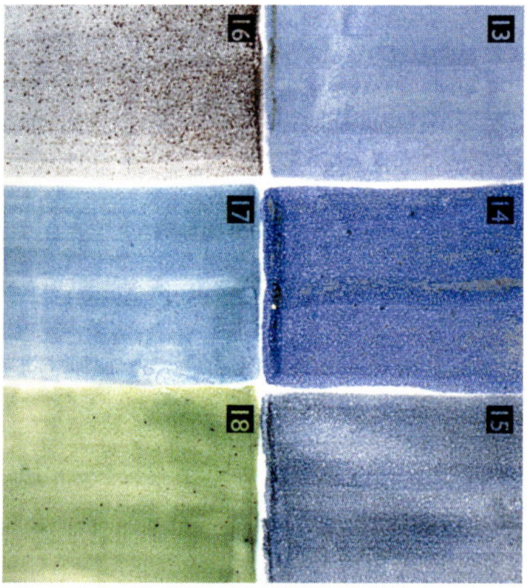

Oxide mixtures 13–18

Colouring oxide mixtures

REF.	Cobalt oxide	Copper oxide	Manganese dioxide	Red iron oxide	Nickel oxide	Rutile	Ilmenite coarse unseived	Chromium oxide	Borax frit	Lead bisilicate	Colour
1						1				2	ochre yellow
2				1		3				3	orange rust
3				2	1				2		tobacco brown
4			1			1.5			2		mushroom brown
5	1			1				0.5	2		blue-black
6		0.5	1						0.5		grey-green
7		1									blue-green
8	1	1	0.5	0.5					2		dark blue-green
9		1				2			2		lustrous green
10		0.5		2					1		bronze green
11					1				1		khaki
12	1								1		strong blue
13	1					2			2		textured blue-grey
14	1						2		2		speckled strong blue
15	1				0.5				1		darkish grey blue
16	0.25		1.5						1		plum blue
17	1	1.5							1		greeny-blue
18		1			1				1		dark green

For fluxing oxides, such as cobalt (blue), copper (blue-green), manganese (plum to brown) and iron (reddy brown), try:

1 part oxide
1 frit
½–1 bentonite (by volume)

For more refractory oxides, such as chrome (grass green), rutile (ochre) and titanium (ivory), or for stains and underglazes, try:

1 part oxide
2–3 frit
½–1 bentonite (by volume)

Arbuckle uses Ferro frit 3124. Borax frit could also be used, or, in the case of iron and rutile, lead bisilicate, as this will give a better colour. Be sure to mix all the ingredients dry, including the bentonite, before adding water and sieving.

Other common painting mediums added to the pigments are laundry starch (1 tbsp per 100 g) for hardness, and glycerine for flow (about 1 tsp per 100 g – dilute in water before use). A solution of SCMC glaze binder (an organic cellulose gum) can also be used. Mix ½ tablespoon to 1 litre water and leave for 24 hours (or follow supplier instructions). Some practitioners prefer to use the oxides on their own (with water) to give greater sensitivity to thickness of application, although frit still needs to be added to

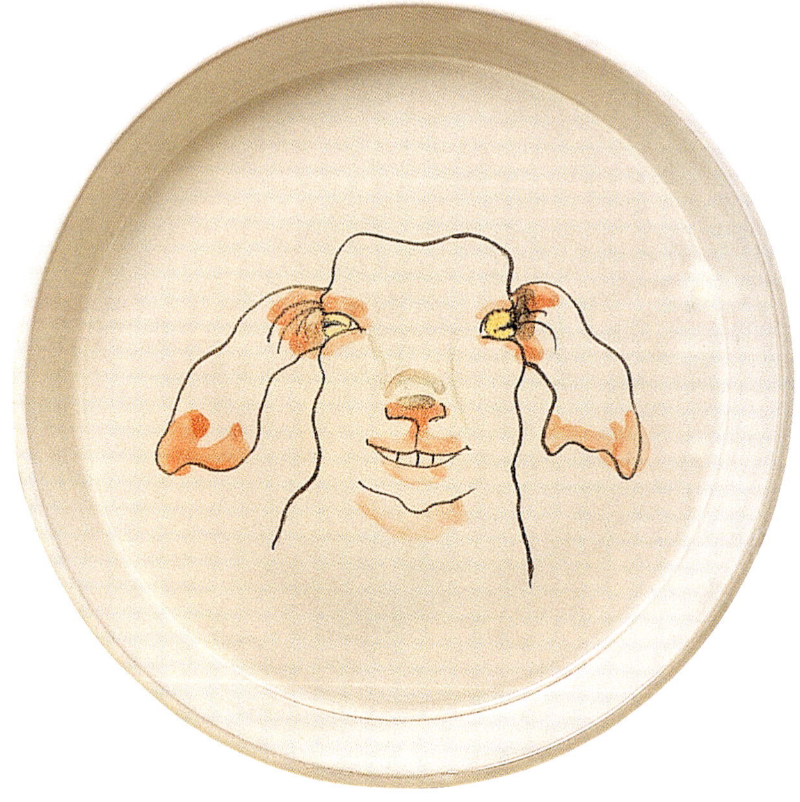

Sheira – the Anglo-Nubian goat, plate by Keiko Hattori, 2004. Dia: 30 cm (11¾ in.). In-glaze painting with stains on lead-based, zircon-opacified glaze. *Photo courtesy of the artist.*

the more refractory pigments. Pigments can be mixed up in liquid form and kept in a container. Alternatively, they can be ground with water on a tile using a palette knife. Gum arabic can be added to improve the flow of the mixture. This should be mixed up in the ratio of 1 cup of water to 3 tbsp of gum arabic powder, boiled and sieved to the consistency of double cream and stored in the dark to prevent it from going off. The pigments are then applied from the tile, like watercolours.

Colouring oxide mixtures

On page 35 is a table of various oxide mixture tests, with the results shown on test tiles. The proportions are given by volume and not by weight, and are painted on the LB4 glaze (see p.100).

Stain mixtures

My standard procedure for stains and underglaze colours is as follows:

Put 1 dessertspoon of powdered stain or underglaze in a container. Pour in either some transparent glaze (I use CTM's G14) or base maiolica glaze until the powder is brought into a thick, creamy mixture. Then add water until the desired painting consistency and flow is achieved. The addition of glaze to the colourant gives extra substance and texture – colours will be somewhat

RIGHT Stain mixtures

A	**Deep turquoise**	
	Persian turquoise	1
	Copper oxide	0.5
B	**Egg yellow**	
	Orange	1
	Lemon yellow	2
	Rutile	1
C	**Burgundy**	
	Cherry red	1
	Turquoise	0.25
D	**Iron red**	
	Poppy red	1
	Red iron oxide	0.25
E	**Mauve**	
	Cherry red	1
	Cobalt oxide	0.25
F	**Orange**	
	Rosso red	0.5
	Lemon yellow	1
G	**Yellowy orange**	
	Lemon yellow	1
	Poppy red	0.25
	Rutile	0.25
H	**Lime green**	
	Yellow	1
	Turquoise	0.5

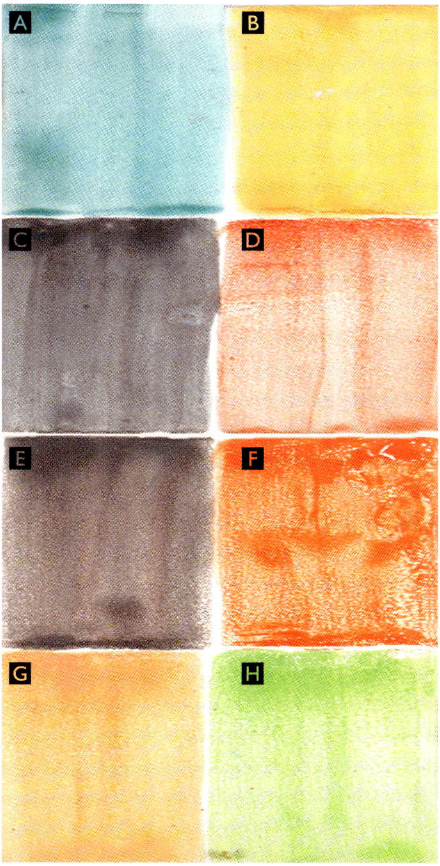

stronger with the transparent glaze. Where colourants are intermixed with either glaze or frit, sometimes sieving through an 80s mesh test sieve will be necessary.

Stains can be intermixed either with other stains or with oxides. I often alter the proportions and try new combinations. Above are some examples of stain mixtures, also by volume, and prepared as described above with transparent glaze.

Firing

Traditionally maiolica was fired in a wood-fired kiln, with the glazed wares protected from the blistering flames and the fly-ash in saggars. Most practitioners today use electric kilns, to which there are obvious advantages – they are reliable, computer controlled, and leave the maker free to get on with other tasks.

Tin-glazed earthenware has always been twice-fired. This is because tin glazes, being of a high viscosity, have a tendency to crawl if used in raw-firing. The traditional industrial and continental procedure is to fire the bisque higher than the glost. With a high lime body, this ensures that the clay is fired to its maturing point, giving a tighter, stronger, more craze-proof body. The lower glost temperature also ensures maximum colour response and stability of glaze and colour, and the process in general allows ware likely to warp to be supported during firing.

Practitioners using standard red bodies with wider firing ranges tend to reverse the above procedure, carrying out a lower biscuit firing to approximately 1000°C (1832°F) followed by a higher glaze firing, usually in the range of 1040–1140°C (1904–2084°F). Due to their viscosity, maiolica glazes have a very wide firing range, with the opportunity for a range of heat-related surface qualities and degrees of opacity to be attempted.

The biscuit firing should be carried out at no more than 100°C per hour up to 1000°C (1832°F). A body with high carbon and sulphur content may need to be fired slightly higher, more slowly, or with a longer soak to enable all the organic matter – which might cause white-spotting or pin-holing in the subsequent glaze firing – to be completely cleared.

Glaze firing of maiolica should also not be rushed, as viscous glazes benefit greatly from a long, slow firing, particularly in the latter part of the climb. A soak also helps the glaze to smooth out and eliminate pin-holes, and gives it a lustrous finish. The firing schedule I follow is as follows:

150°C/302°F per hr up to 850°C/1562°F
100°C/212°F per hr up to 1080°C/1976°F
30 minute soak

In my kiln, this is equivalent to Orton Cone 02. Pyrometric cones record heatwork, and it is important to use them, as they can record the temperature differentials in various parts of the kiln as well as ensuring consistency from one firing to the next. In addition, if a glaze firing has been aborted (due, say, to a power cut or a faulty kiln element), the same cone should be used for refiring to ensure the correct glaze maturity is reached.

Sometimes, a refire will be necessary to touch up crawled patches or add more colour etc. This should always be to a lower temperature (say 20°C lower) than that of the original glaze firing, or else the glaze will become over-fired with adverse results.

Sintering

Sintering is an intermediate glaze firing in which the glaze is fired only up to a point where the surface is hard, no longer powdery and yet can still absorb the pigments. This means that fine details and washes of colour can be carried out more easily without risk of disturbing the glaze. Sintering is also advantageous for more complex decorative processes such as those used by Marshall Colman (see p 84)and Lisa Katzenstein (see p 91). Once the decoration is complete, the piece is fired again up to the normal glaze maturing temperature.

A glaze is sintered when a reaction has begun between the solids in the glaze, causing the particles to stick together without allowing actual melting to take place. Porosity is decreased, and the strength of the surface is increased. Those practitioner's more scientifically inclined should refer to Michael Cardew's book *Pioneer Pottery* (London, Longman 1969), in which he describes a method of calculating the exact sintering point of a glaze. For those of us who work more empirically, a few firing tests should be sufficient to find the correct sintering point for your glaze – usually somewhere in the region of cone 018 to cone 015, depending on the final maturing temperature of your glaze.

Chapter 3

Surface treatment

Undecorated maiolica

Conventionally, tin-glazed earthenware has been used as a foundation for applied colour. There is, however, also a long tin glaze tradition of unadorned glaze with little or no pigment decoration, as exemplified in the French and Italian 16th and 17th century whitewares (*faience blanche, bianchi di Faenza*) and some simple utilitarian English Delftware pieces, such as posset pots and wine bottles. These were relatively humble pieces, reliant on form, the surface quality of the glaze and sometimes relief texture for effect. This use of tin glaze use is echoed in the work of the Swiss ceramicist Margrit Linck (1897–1983). Her thrown and distorted *Weisse Vasen* with their archaic, reductive references to human forms exploit the qualities of a white tin glaze for its ability to enhance form.

The contemporary, functional work of Kate Scott also includes the use of plain tin-glazed pieces, punctuated by simple, fine, slip-trailed lines which provide subtle, understated relief interest. These are done at the leather-hard stage with a fairly fine nozzle, and need to be rubbed down a bit after the biscuit firing. The glaze firing is to cone 1 – high enough for the red clay to burn warmly through the glaze on the trailed lines, rims and edges.

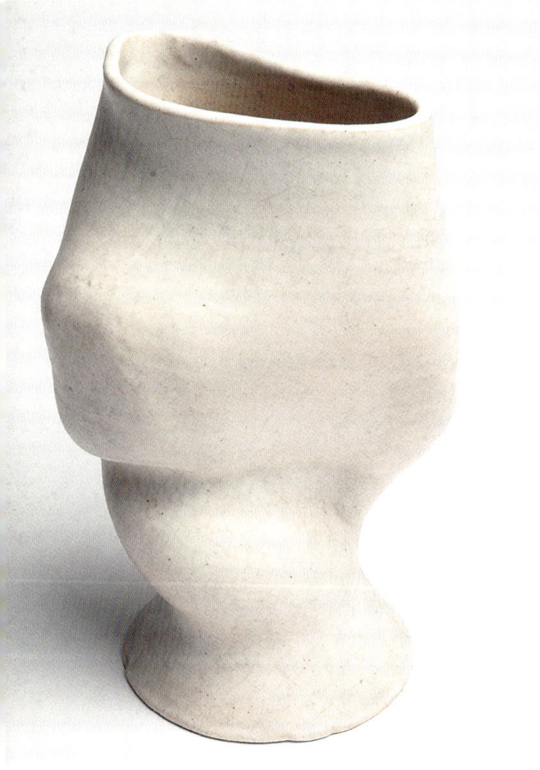

Brushes and brushwork

Brushwork is really the life-blood of maiolica. Its use goes right back to 9th century Mesopotamia, when Islamic potters set a precedent for strong and lively brush decoration. The whiteness of the glaze represents an irresistible invitation to colourful mark-making,

Vase by Margrit Linck, 1980. Ht: 24 cm (9½ in.). Matt tin glaze. *Collection of Veronica Norburn. Photo by Naomi Schillinger.*

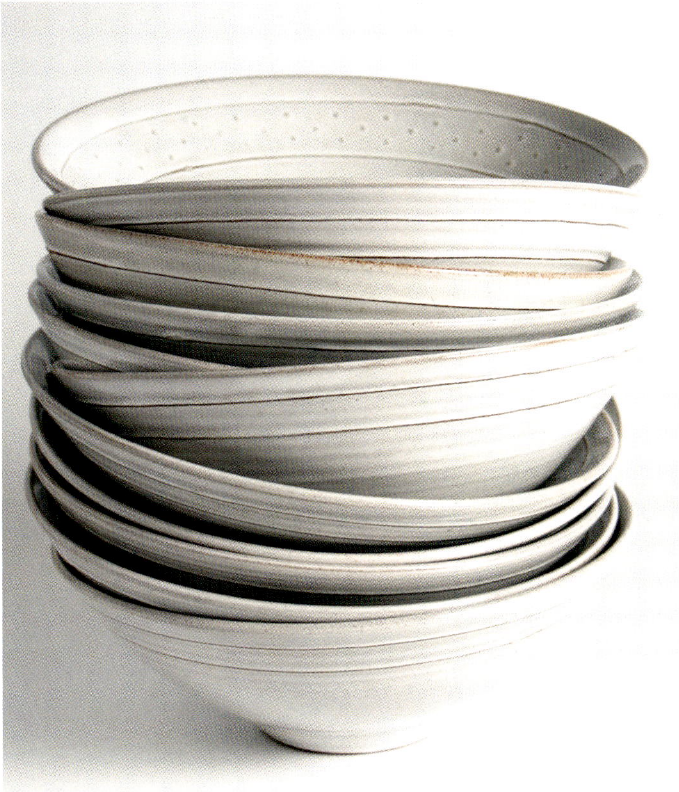

Bowls by Kate Scott. Dia: 20 cm (8 in.). *Photo courtesy of the artist.*

and applying colour with a brush is the most immediate way of doing this. This mark-making can radically affect the way we perceive both the form and the spirit of a piece. Alan Caiger-Smith describes painted decoration as an exploration of form, just as 'bare feet discover the sand'. Similarly, Andrea Gill refers to the maiolica glaze as being 'like a loose skin on a body', ripe for further transformation through painted colour and pattern.

Styles of painting

Looking at both historical and contemporary styles of maiolica painting, they can be roughly separated into two broad categories of brush usage. The first can be called 'calligraphic' or 'gestural' – in the sense that the content and manner of the painting take their cue from the quality of the brushstroke itself. In short, the shape and character of the stroke is a main component of the design.

Alan Caiger-Smith's work epitomises the calligraphic approach. He is, by his own definition, primarily concerned with 'formalised movement and abstraction'. As with the Islamic and Hispano-Moresque pots whose generosity and energy first aroused his interest in tin glaze, he is striving for an endlessly exciting and rhythmic 'dance' by means of an open-ended calligraphic language. For him, the starting points of any work are colour and the power of the brush. He spent years learning the language of each type of brush, finding out what each was

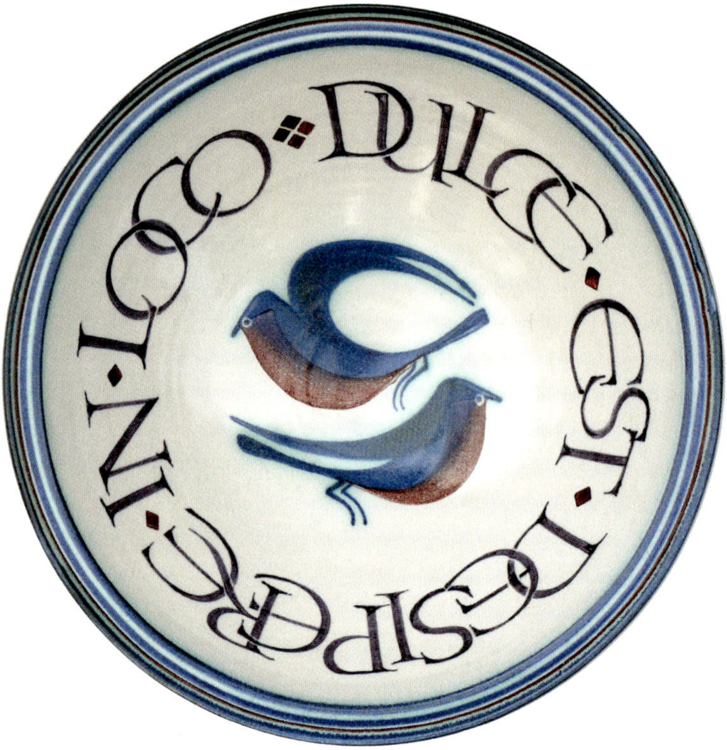

Rimmed bowl, by Laurence McGowan, 2006. Stoneware maiolica. Dia: 25 cm (9¾ in.). Inscription from Horace 'How sweet it is to relax at the proper time'. *Photo by Jackie McGowan.*

capable of. He also came to the realisation that some ideas were impossible to carry out because they were not sympathetic to the expressions of the brush. Caiger-Smith's personal preferences are manifest in his work by way of underlying, but well-assimilated, historical references – both in the calligraphic style, as well as in the use of reduced lustre on-glaze decoration, (see illustration p.81).

Laurence McGowan also works in calligraphic style, but on a high-fired, stoneware tin glaze.

> My work, whilst not being imitative, doubtless reflects my interest in both the aims and influences of the Arts and Crafts movement and Islamic design traditions. I am essentially a pattern maker, applying two dimensional patterns in a way which attempts to reflect the three-dimensional character of the pot. My motifs are stylised forms taken from nature. They are intended as reminders or evocations of things rather than in any way literal. The decoration, including the lettering, is done using chisel ended brushes of various sizes, supplemented with a few pointed ones.

Stanley Mace Andersen and Linda Arbuckle, without working in the formally calligraphic way that characterises Caiger-Smith's and McGowan's work, are examples of contemporary maiolica practitioners who work in a direct, gestural manner and exploit the full potential of individual brushstrokes.

The other convention of brush usage is generally more graphic in nature, using brushes as fillers, shaders and liners in the service of a more pictorial vision, and rooted in the European tin glaze tradition. Modern practitioners working in this manner include Hylton Nel, Phyllis Kloda and Reptile (for examples of their work, refer to index). Matthias Ostermann, who sadly died in 2009, also worked in this fashion, and was a master of the illustrative style of painting (see p.51–2 and p.65).

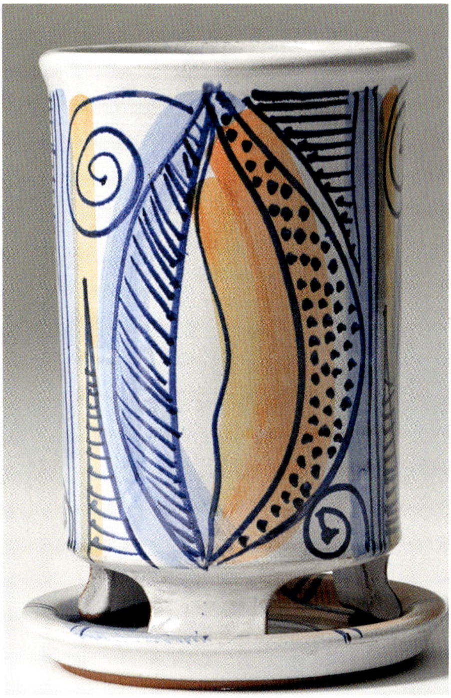

RIGHT Cutlery drainer by Daphne Carnegy. Ht: 17 cm (6¾ in.), 2009. *Photo by Sussie Ahlburg.*

BELOW Square bowl with falling leaves by Linda Arbuckle, 2005. 14 × 23 × 20 cm (5½ × 9 × 8 in.). *Photo courtesy of the artist.*

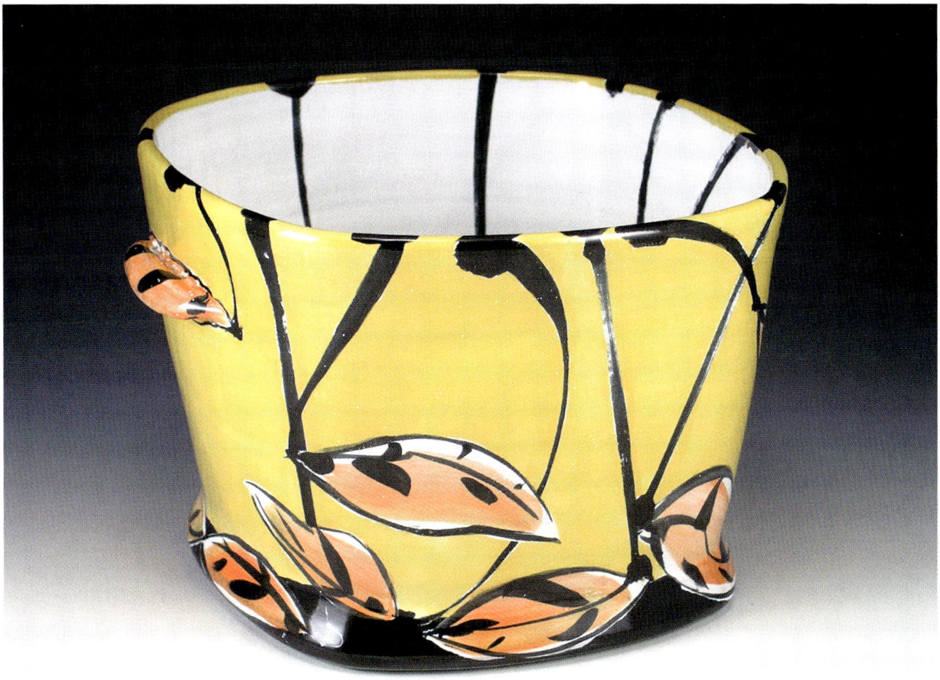

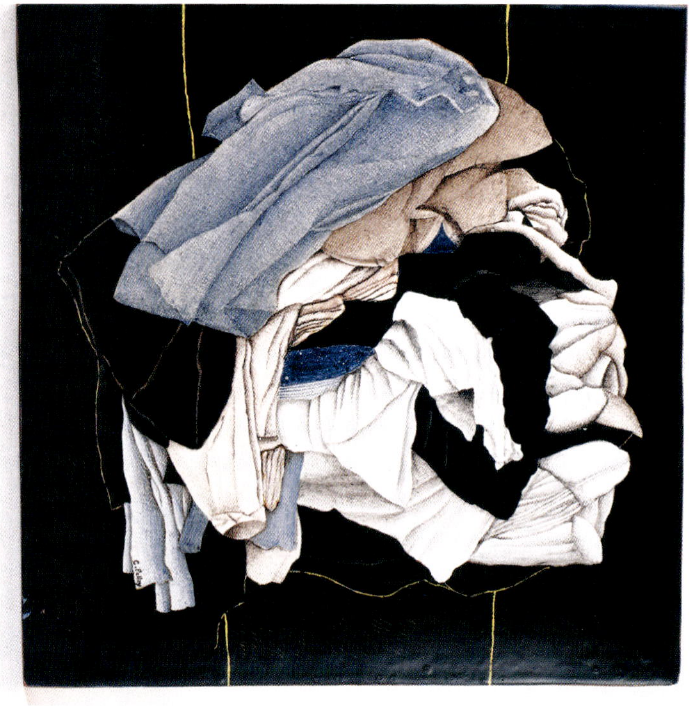

Pile of Washing, tile by Claude and Slavik Palley. 24.5 × 25 cm (9¾ × 10 in.). *Courtesy of the Association des Amis de Claude et Slavik Palley. Photo by Jean Girel.*

The work of Claude and Slavik Palley, whose active production ceased in 1996, is Italianate in its fine detail and skilled use of colour.

There are, of course, a wealth of other painting styles which cannot be categorised in such a clear-cut way; the two cited above are the most commonly encountered.

Brushes

It is important to find brushes that match your intentions – which ones you choose ultimately depend on what they will do for you, or on what you want to do with them. Painting can be a real struggle with inappropriate or inadequate brushes, and finding just the right one can make all the difference to your final result.

Appropriate brushes could mean anything from decorators' paintbrushes to the finest sable – it all depends on what you need. One important factor for all brushes, however, is their ability to hold colour – you do not want to run out of colour in the middle of a gestural brushstroke! Shape, size and degree of softness or hardness are also to be considered. Soft brushes are less likely to disturb the glaze surface, but hard (e.g. bristle) brushes can be useful for wet-blending the colours on the glaze surface (as in Ostermann's work).

Chinese or Japanese calligraphy brushes are excellent for variable brushstrokes, and for using flat (as 'blobs', or extended blobs). Watercolour brushes are good general purpose brushes. I regularly use synthetic (nylon) watercolour brushes for this purpose –

one-strokes as fillers or for calligraphic strokes, scriptliners for fine detail, outlines, and 'stabbing' strokes. They are virtually indestructible, hold colour well, and have a good level of resilience.

Other brushes worth trying are sign-writing and ticket-writing brushes, coach liners, artists' varnishing brushes, and specialist wood-graining and marbling brushes. I usually have duplicates or even triplicates of those brushes I use most often, so that they can be used for different colour groups (e.g. the blues, the greens or the yellows/oranges) without having to rinse so thoroughly each time.

All brushes should be well looked after. Rinse them well after use, and then leave them to dry on their sides so that water does not soak into the handle (especially important for bamboo-handled brushes). Never use your good brushes to stir up your colours, and never leave them point-down in water; these things can ruin their shapes very easily. Also, if a brush becomes loose in its metal holder over time, hammer the metal case so that it grips the brush more tightly – this will keep a good brush in use for much longer.

Strategies and preparation for painting

It can be a terrifying moment when you are confronted with the white expanse of a glazed piece, and are ready with a brush poised. For those new to painting in this way, I would recommend these two principles:

- Follow the form
- Exploit the qualities of your brushes

Take your cue for design from the form of your piece. If you look at the earliest Italian 'archaic' maiolica jugs

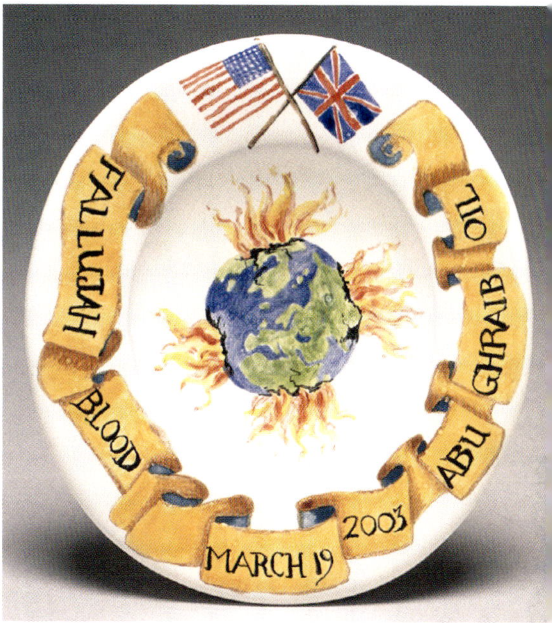

Dish by Walter Ostrom, 2004. *Photo by Julian Beveridge Photographic.*

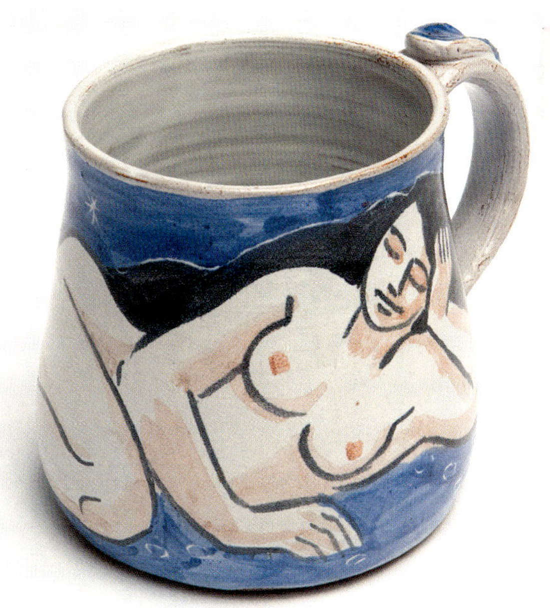

Mug by Lucy Rickards, 2008. Ht: 9 cm (3½ in.). Rickards works from her life-drawings, translating them into the maiolica medium. *Photo by Naomi Schillinger.*

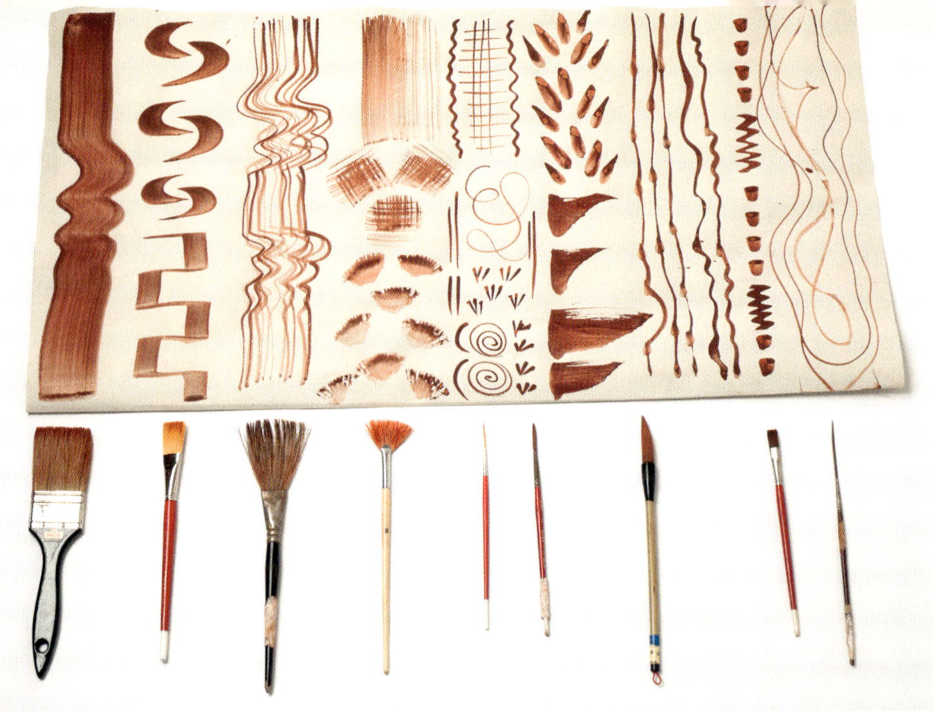

Brushstrokes on paper, with their respective brushes. Left to right: decorator's brush, medium one-stroke, wood-grainer, fan, scriptliners, Chinese brush, small one-stroke, coach liner. *Photo by Naomi Schillinger.*

with composite forms, great fat beaks and wide strappy handles, the simple geometric decoration in manganese and copper which they use is highly effective in articulating the form. The form has dictated the placing of the brushstrokes: a fat, round jar, for example, might suggest the use of full, rounded motifs; a free-form dish might suggest flowing, gestural brushstrokes in sympathy with the profile. To a certain extent, forms should be created with an idea of the intended focus of the decoration, how it will accommodate to the surface, and how it physically can be carried out. Will you be able to easily access the areas you wish to paint, for instance? Always bear in mind how different drawing a 2D decorative design in your sketchbook can be from actually executing it on a 3D surface.

With regard to fully exploiting the brushes, it is essential to try out your repertoire of brushstrokes on a large piece of paper – at least A3 size. This allows you to try out each brush in turn, see what they will do, and experiment with them in a variety of ways. This process also helps you to loosen up and build confidence for when you come to paint the real thing. In general, use your whole arm to create flowing and generous brushmarks. Test to find the amount of pressure required for a sustained, flowing stroke – it is often much lighter than you would think. Similarly, learn to enjoy the variations in density of colour within a brushstroke – dark and strong at the beginning, and fading out at the end. Brushwork is all about a combination of confidence and control!

The raw glaze readily absorbs the colour from the brush, and the nature, speed and load of the brushstroke are instantly registered as expressive, painterly marks on the fired surface. These are qualities special to maiolica. It is not a forgiving technique, however, so every mark which you make will be visible. Any hesitancy or tightness in the use of the brush will be only too obvious in the finished piece. Just go for it! Over time, you will greatly improve – the more you do it, the better it gets.

Before starting to paint, make sure you have everything to hand – pigments, brushes, water, glaze for touching up, a palette knife for correcting errors, your sketchbook for reference, etc. When I paint, I also have a glazed 'tester' piece available so that I can test the consistency of the pigments prior to application.

It is important to position yourself correctly according to the kind of piece you are painting. Bowls and dishes, for example, can be placed on a bubblewrap disc on a bat on the wheelhead. This ensures there is no damage caused to the glaze on the rim if you are decorating the underside. Small bowls and mugs can be held in the hand, whereas larger pieces such as vases and jugs are best decorated at eye level.

Prior to actual painting, I wipe the bases and feet of all the pieces, fettle any glaze dribbles which would interfere with the painting, and touch up tong scar marks. I also rub over any cracks in the glaze where it has collected and which could cause crawling in the firing. These are usually awkward places, such as where a handle meets the pot.

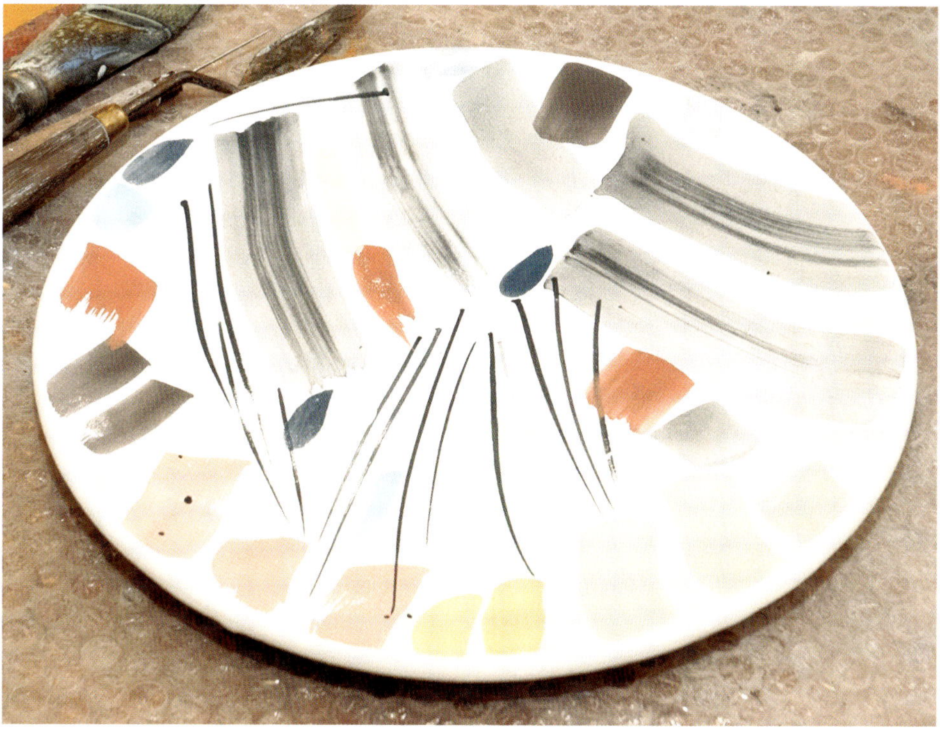

'Tester' plate (unfired) for testing colour thickness. The bubble wrap is to protect the rims of bowls and plates when decorating the underside. *Photo by Naomi Schillinger.*

Daphne Carnegy painting techniques

Agapanthus design

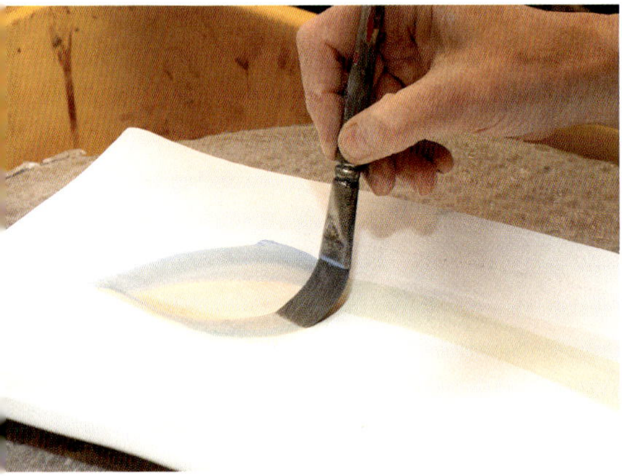

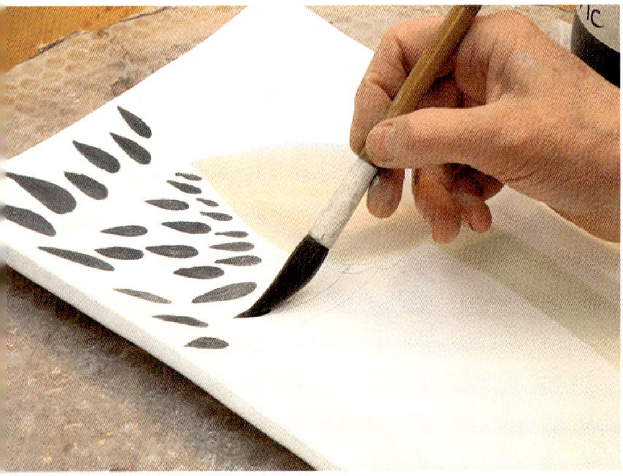

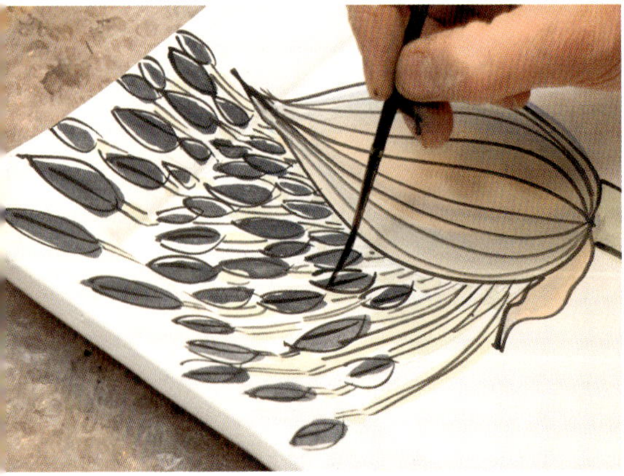

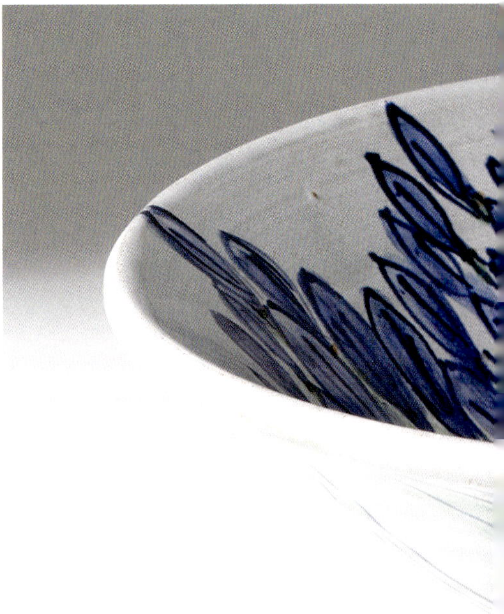

ABOVE Bowl with agapanthus design by Daphne Carnegy. Dia: 22 cm (8¾ in.). *Photo by Sussie Ahlburg.*

LEFT, FROM TOP After sketching out a rough design in soft pencil, brown yellow, green and blue pigments are layered and shaded using a wide one-stroke brush.

Using Chinese brush to make 'posed blobs' for flower head.

Outlining and detailing using scriptliner. *Photos by Naomi Schillinger.*

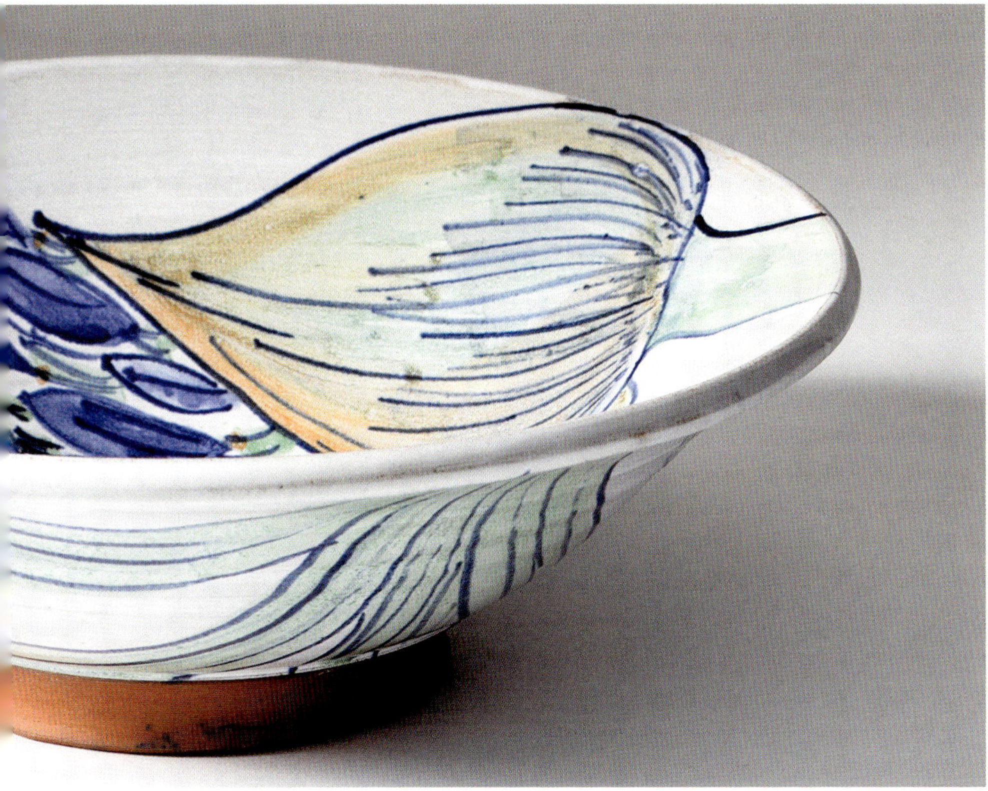

Pear design with dark background

The sequence is similar to that of the agapanthus design, but with some dry blending on the pear itself and a dark background.

BELOW, LEFT Dry blending the layered yellow, green and iron red pigments.

BELOW After outlining, the background is carefully painted on with a one-stroke brush. *Photos by Naomi Schillinger.*

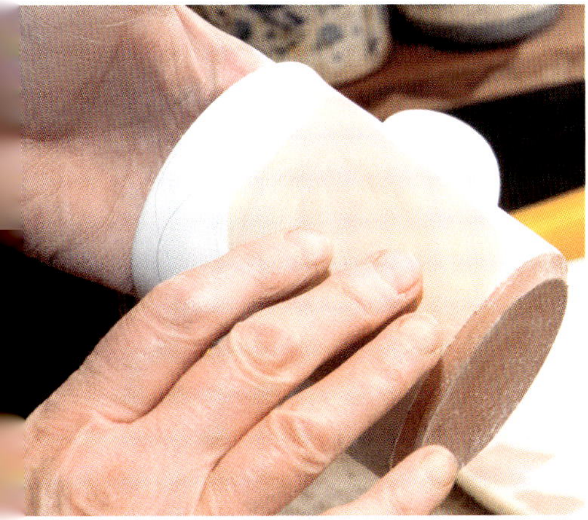

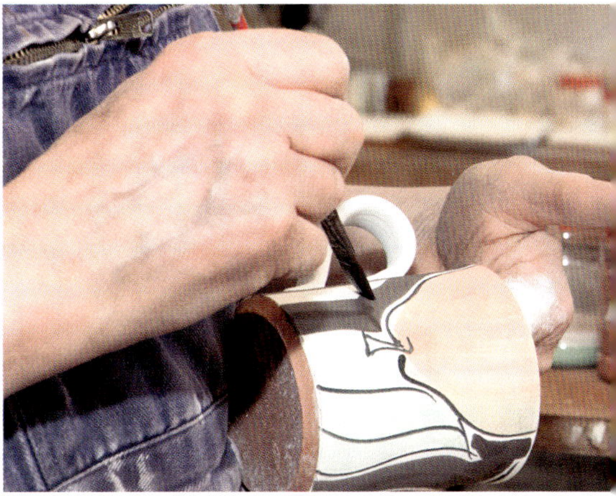

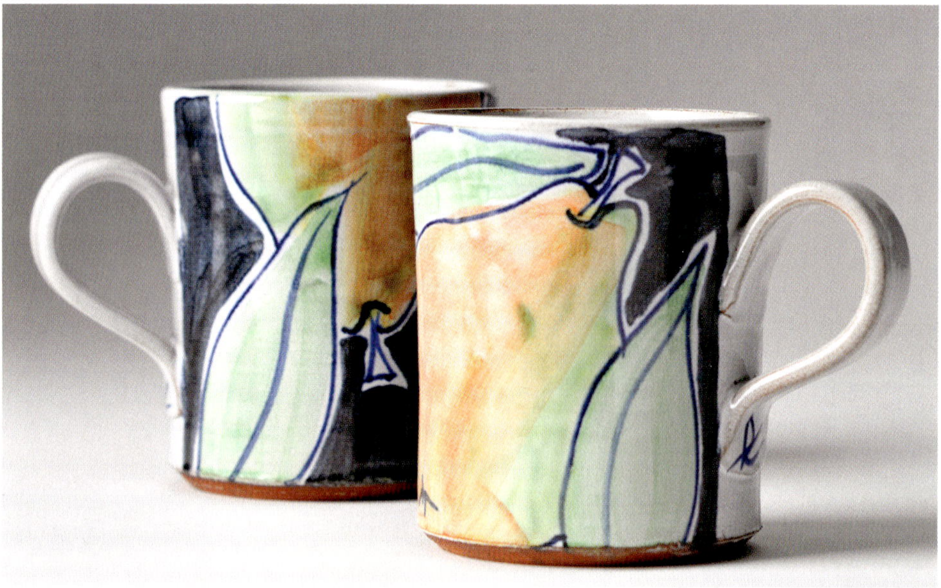

Fired mugs by Daphne Carnegy. *Photo by Sussie Ahlburg.*

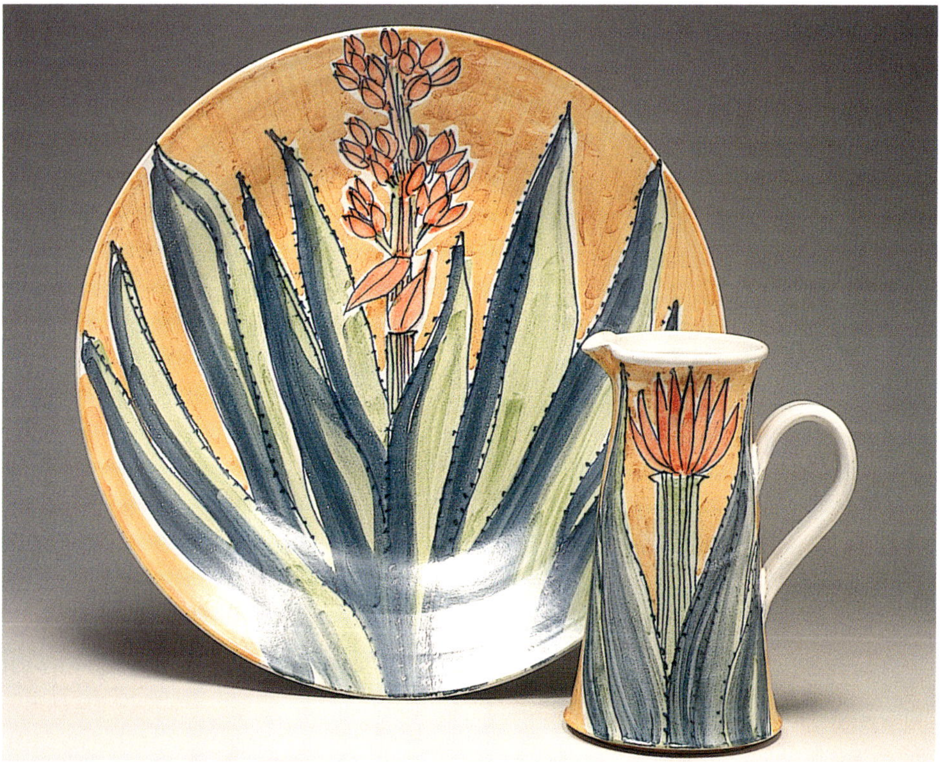

Dish and jug by Daphne Carnegy, 2004. Dia (dish): 38 cm (15 in.). *Photo by Stephen Brayne.*

Matthias Ostermann (1951–2009) began using maiolica in the 1980s after a study tour of Italy, and he committed himself to this technique despite the long-standing prejudice against earthenware which existed in North America at the time. He became known worldwide for his highly skilled maiolica ceramics and for his great knowledge in the field, which culminated in his book *The New Maiolica*. His work is characterised by an intensity and richness of palette, in which colours are built up and blended. This method not only covers the whole surface, but also creates a feeling of depth not dissimilar to that of an oil painting – but with the added qualities of light penetration which are inherent in maiolica. The colours have been blended to a personal palette using mostly commercial stains. Borax frit is then added – more or less according to the degree of surface gloss required (one to one of borax frit and stain mixed together is a standard melt). The density of the colour, ranging from translucent watercolour to thick oil-paint effects, depends on the amount of water used to dilute the pigment.

Ostermann used a wide range of painting techniques, all executed with great skill and flair. As he described:

> a brush is one of the most intimate and gestural of all tools – it becomes an extension of our own body. Brushwork reflects not only the artist's intent in presenting an image, but also his or her ability to meld fluid and controlled gesture into concrete expression, be it line, wash or colour blending. (Ostermann, op.cit.)

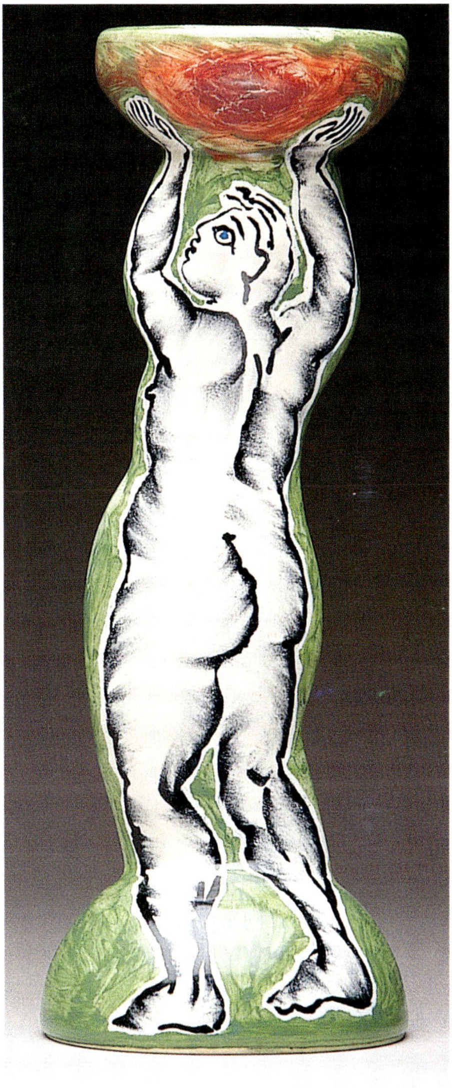

Atlas candleholder by Matthias Ostermann, 1997. Ht: 26 cm (10¼ in.). *Photo by Jan Thujs.*

For the rich, dense coloured designs, stains and oxides are applied in layers with a soft, full brush. These are then either blended on the surface with a stiff, not-too-wet, round-tipped brush using deliberate directional strokes to create surface movement, or are dry blended for a softer effect. Next, a fine black line contour drawing is superimposed onto the image with a fine-pointed

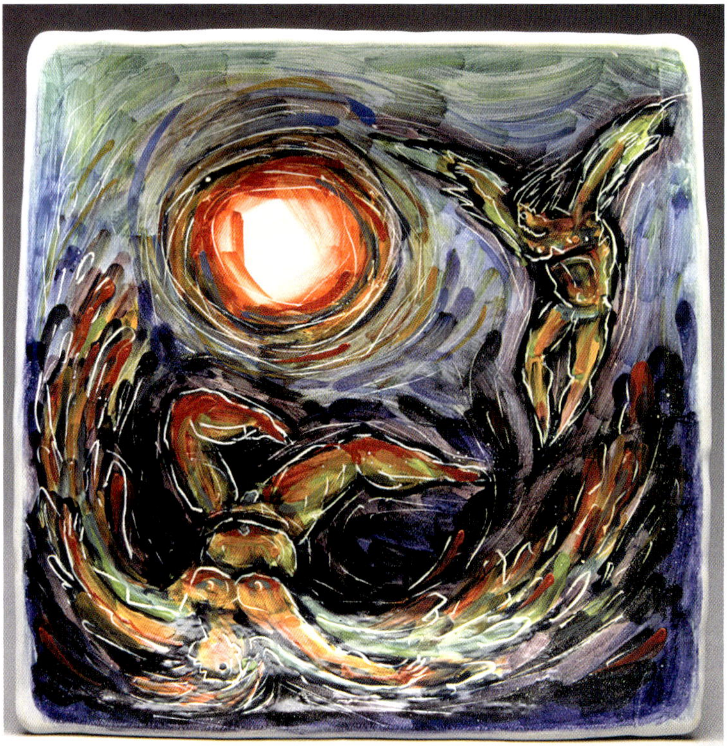

Icarus wall plate by Matthias Ostermann, 2003. W: 33 cm (13 in.). *Photo by Jan Thujs. Courtesy of Daniel Grummisch.*

calligraphy brush, followed by quick, light sgraffito lines through the colour to create added definition. Sometimes, a black outline is smudged with a finger to create an effect of volume or movement. A more airy effect can be achieved by means of fluid, deft, economical brushstrokes on a white background.

Ostermann Maiolica Glaze no.1
(cone 05)

Ferro frit 3124	60
Ferro frit 3195	10
Ball clay	6.5
EPK (china clay)	6.5
Flint	4
Whiting	2
Zircopax	11

Ostermann Maiolica Glaze no.2
(cone 1–2)

Ferro frit 3124	62
Ball clay	9
EPK (china clay)	9
Flint	6
Whiting	3
Zircopax	11

Linda Arbuckle's pieces are functional, seek to be 'happy and indulgent', and are decorated with gestural brushwork.

The functional vessel brings experiences through the useful art object into one's daily life. Line, colour, gesture and the lure of materiality articulate the value of indulgence and the transience of (plant) life. The alchemy that transforms common terracotta clay into a resonant object in a domestic setting points the way towards parallel transformations possible in the observed moments of personal life.

Her influences are numerous, and include Japanese art, Minoan and Mimbres ceramics, Far Eastern and European ceramics, textiles, wallpaper, animals and plants. Pieces are thrown, thrown-and-altered, or hump-moulded with hand-built additions, and are characterised by their strong, vibrant colours. She makes her own terracotta bodies with the addition of barium carbonate to neutralise the adverse effects of magnesium and calcium sulphates (salts). Biscuit firing is to cone 05.

Arbuckle majolica recipe (cone 03)	
Ferro frit 3124	65.8
Kona F-4 feldspar (UK use Cornish Stone)	17.3
EPK (china clay)	10.8
Nepheline syenite	6.2
+ Bentonite	2
+ Tin oxide	4
+ Zircopax	8

Pigments used are Amaco GDC decorating colours, or stains and oxides mixed with Ferro frit 3124 and bentonite (see p.36).

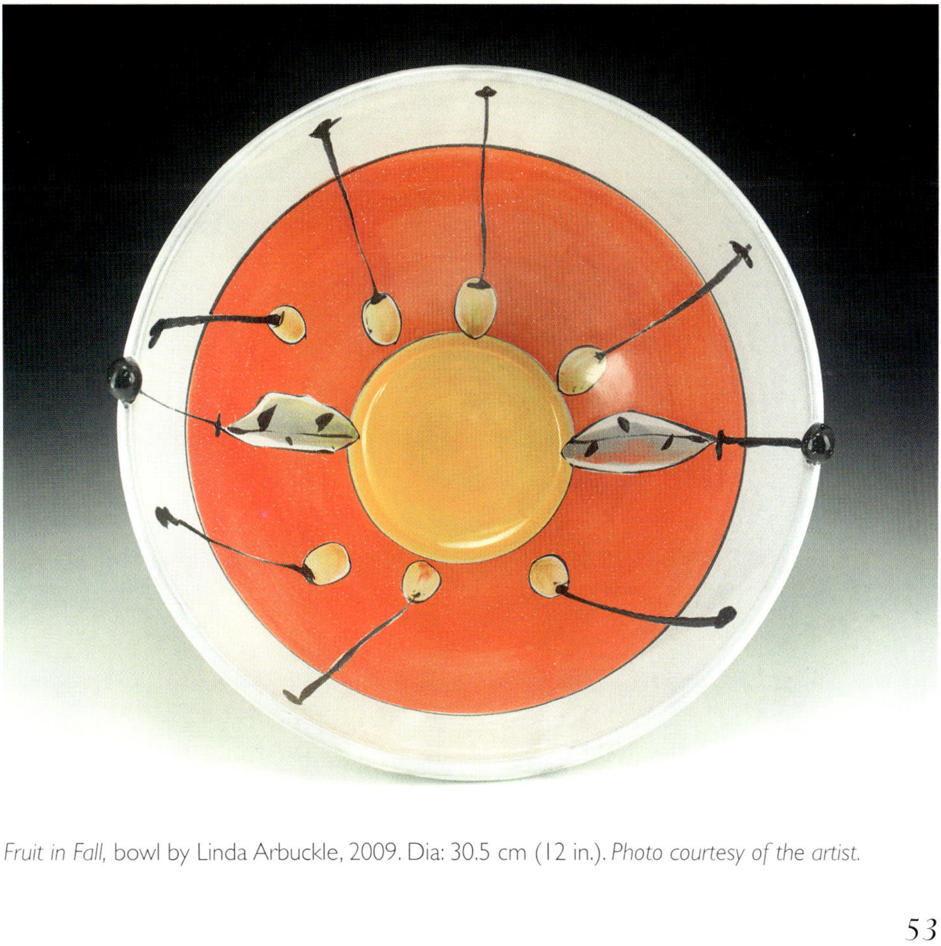

Fruit in Fall, bowl by Linda Arbuckle, 2009. Dia: 30.5 cm (12 in.). *Photo courtesy of the artist.*

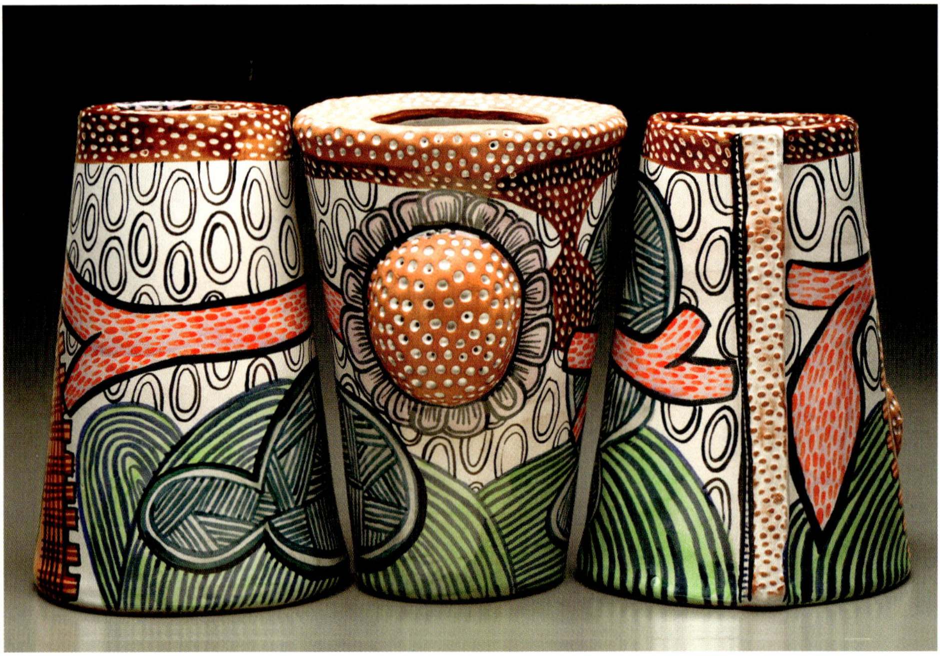

Vase set by Megan Bogonovich, 40 x 21 x12 cm (15¾ x 8¼ x 4¾ in.). '…the groupings are thought of as single artworks, with drawn elements making visual connections from one form to the next…'. *Photo by Charlie Frieberg.*

Megan Bogonovich

> I believe in invasive decoration. Much too much. Lots of colour and lots of pattern. It is decoration that will jump from one piece to the next, without considering the expectations of the functional form. Playful and bossy decoration. ... The majolica drawing is unplanned, I make decisions as I work, so often my mood or the aesthetics of my day will shape the patterning. I think of each piece as an opportunity to make a unique and spontaneous drawing.

Bogonovich uses a red earthenware body to make her slab-built pieces. Paper patterns and hump moulds are used to create uniformity, and textured additions are pinched and detailed with simple tools. Inspiration for her surface designs comes from a variety of sources – sea-life, flora and fauna, fabric and textile designs and cartoon style.

Both biscuit and glaze firing are to cone 03. For her maiolica in-glaze painting, she uses pre-mixed Amaco decorating colours – sometimes layering the colours for more complexity. Relief areas have glaze applied and then wiped back to enhance their texture and give contrast with the other, conventionally glazed areas. She also carves back into colours to re-expose the base white glaze and uses thin washes of colour to alter the existing pre-mixed colours. Outlining is a salient feature of her work as well, and she has a favourite brush for this purpose which can make a long thin line and hold a lot of pigment.

Reptile

Reptile is the name of the company comprised of Carlo Briscoe and Edward Dunn. Tin-glazed earthenware is the perfect medium for a range of finely executed, illustrative tiles and tile panels. The subject matter of the design may arise in response to a commission, but is often inspired by the natural world – fish, birds and animals. The influence of Portuguese, Dutch and English tiles is evident, but references to old European embroideries (e.g. stumpwork) are also present. They use a low temperature, white earthenware body from Commercial clays to make their hand-rolled tiles. These are then dried between factory-made biscuit tiles to prevent warping. Biscuit firing is to 1000°C (1832°F), and glaze firing to 1050°C (1922°F).

The tiles are hand dipped in the glaze and allowed to dry for 1–2 days before painting. Designs are drawn loosely and lightly onto the dry glaze with a 9B pencil. Reptile produce many ranges of

Coffee, tile panel by Reptile. Tiles are 15 × 15 cm (6 × 6 in.) square. Painted with cobalt oxide, with the lines in dark blue (manganese dioxide 9, cobalt oxide 4, by weight).

tiles, but never use stencils; every tile is totally individual. Some of their tiles have sponged areas on them, which is done first. A banding wheel is used for any circular borders.

All of the colours are mixed with some base glaze. The fine line (with no base glaze added) is painted last of all with a rigger brush.

Pigments used include oxides of cobalt, copper, iron, manganese, nickel, and red, light blue and yellow stains – all mixed with a little of the base glaze. The brushes used are sable brushes from Jackson's and watercolour riggers – number 0 or 00.

Megan Patey, who came to ceramics from a fine art background, is excited by the way maiolica reveals the subtle intricacies of colour mixing and the energy of brush strokes. Shape in her designs is produced by varying the widths of her brushes and brush stroke. Patey uses synthetic sable brushes, and works quickly and with focus – the expressive character of the brushwork is essential to creating life and pattern in her work. Her influences include early Italian and Spanish tin-glazed earthenware, Japanese Oribe ware, and painters such as Picasso and Matisse. She uses a red clay body (Clayworks CTC #60), with biscuit firing done to 1000°C (1832°F) and glaze firing to 1100°C (2012°F).

Patey's maiolica glaze (cone 03–02)	
Ferro frit 4193	70
Nepheline Syenite	10
Ball clay	5
Calcined china clay	5
Silica (flint)	5
Tin (and/or zircon)	10

For her painting, Patey uses a combination of commercial stains (Mason, Blythe), colouring oxides and carbonates. Frit is added to these in varying proportions, according to the degree of fusibility exhibited in the colourants.

In common with watercolour painting, designs are built up using transparent layers. This is then followed by more concentrated applications of colour; pigment concentration is decided by eye, stroking colours onto paper before moving onto the glazed ware.

Steve Davis-Rosenbaum reveals an interesting cultural fusion in his work. Eastern influences are strong, and he has been much inspired by the Japanese Mingei folk-art movement, often referring to his work as 'minge-olica'. This is reflected in his confident style of painting. He uses Amaco GDCs, diluted as needed, Mason stains (1 part stain to 3 parts gerstley borate and 1 part Ferro frit 3124, plus water), and copper and cobalt carbonate (mixed with 1–2 parts gerstley borate plus water). Designs are sketched on to the surface of the pieces using a 4B pencil, and colours brushed on with some multi-layering and blending to give depth. Certain areas of the designs are then outlined in black, and some sgraffito is added to give contrast to the black lines. He uses a custom-made body, biscuit fired to cone 06. The glazes are zircon-opacified glazes based on Ferro frit 3124 and fired to cone 04 (½ to 3 tablespoons of Epsom salts are added to 5 gallons (approx. 20 litres) of glaze).

Square platter by Megan Patey, 24 × 24 cm (9½ × 9½ in.). *Photo by John Lascelles, Mittagong, NSW Australia.*

'This piece uses the white of the glaze as an integral part of the total design, with some scratching gently through the glaze to break up flatness of brush strokes.'

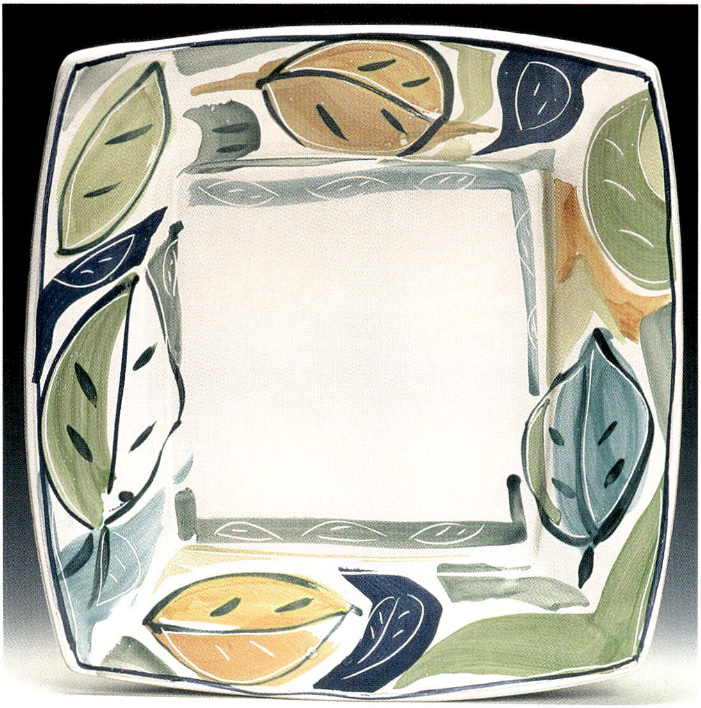

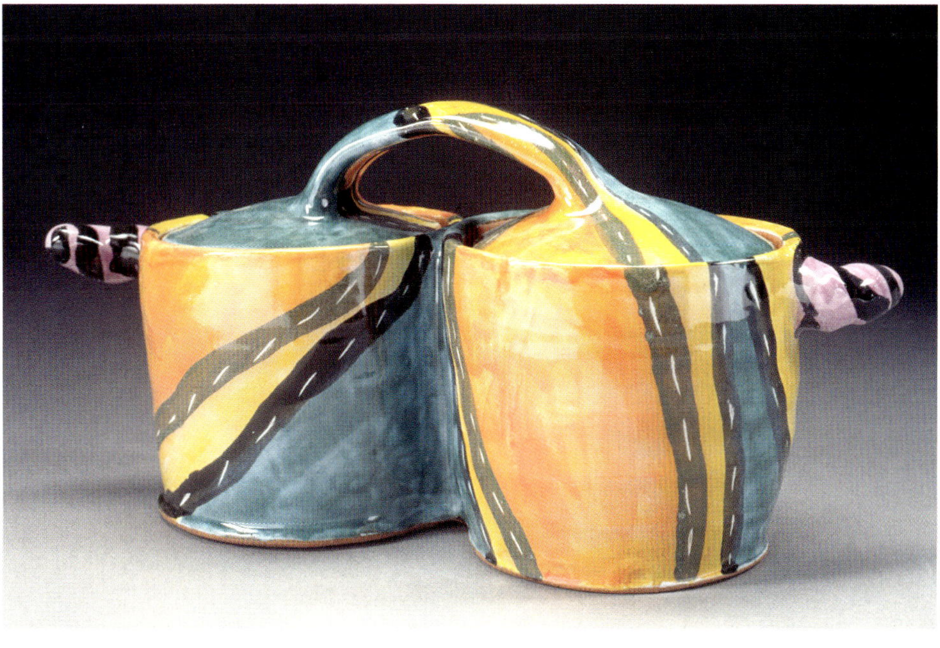

Double-covered jar set, by Steve Davis-Rosenbaum. 10 × 32 cm (4 × 12½ in.). *Photo by Mary Rezny.*

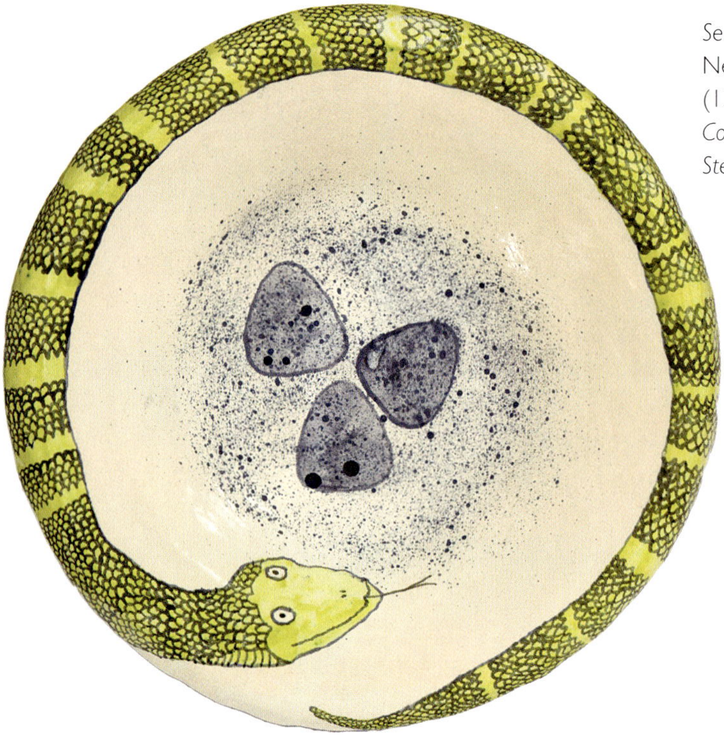

Serpent bowl, by Hylton Nel, 2009. Dia: 33 cm (13 in.), ht: 12cm (4¾in.). *Courtesy of Michael Stevenson, Cape Town.*

Hylton Nel

Michael Stevenson, author of the book *Hylton Nel*, writes:

> Nel describes himself as an 'artist-potter' which aptly refers to his interest in painted imagery as well as with form and function. Over the past four decades he has developed a style of work that is rich in references to the decorative arts and literary and art historical sources. His plates, bowls, vases, plaques and figurative pieces are idiosyncratically decorated with witty – and sometimes poignant – line drawings and script. His imagery ranges from penises to madonnas, and from cats through to angels.

Trained as a fine artist and inspired by Italian maiolica and English and Dutch Delftware, Nel became fascinated by the qualities of tin-glazed earthenware. Of decoration, he says:

> The different way that the drawings [are arrived at] often has to do with the pigment I'm using – with how it actually flows, because remember these things are painted on a raw, glazed surface, so it's powdery. Different pigments flow or don't flow – sometimes they don't flow, and so you struggle with the brush to get the mark made. And then sometimes it flows easily and everything works.

The painting is economical with lines, and is generally restrained, with a relaxed character which speaks of European country traditions. There is also a pleasingly rough-hewn quality to his pieces, far removed from the 'perfection' of mass-produced ceramics.

Stanley Mace Andersen makes distinctive, functional maiolica, having initially begun his ceramic career with porcelain. He greatly enjoys using colour, line and abstract motifs, aiming for these elements to become an integral and harmonious part of the pots. He tries to create a feeling of informality and exuberance with his brushwork.

> There was something about the medium [of maiolica] that lightened my hand. From the start, my decoration on earthenware was less serious – less sombre than anything I had done on porcelain (*Studio Potter* vol.11, no.2, 1983).

Andersen makes his own clay body, and his pieces are mostly thrown. Biscuit firing is to cone 05.

Andersen glaze recipe (cone 03)

Ferro frit 3124	60
OM#4 ball clay	15
Flint	15
Zircopax	7

For pigments, he uses mostly Mason stains and copper carbonate. He uses these colourants in their unmodified, pure states, adding only some glaze frit to the mix of water and stain. This mixture is pretty much done by eye – a spoonful of frit to a spoonful of stain. No other additives are used. He paints directly and fairly quickly on the raw glaze surface, exploiting the inherent qualities of his brushes with no special surface preparation or under-drawing. Over the years, he has expanded his decorating repertoire to include more overlapping and layering of a wider range of colours.

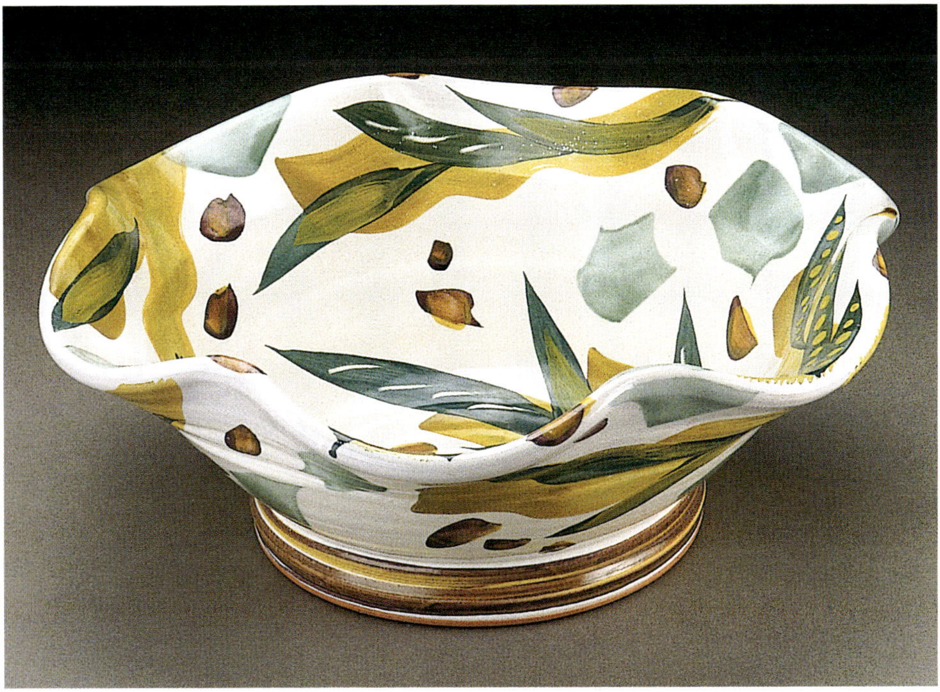

Serving bowl by Stanley Mace Andersen. Dia: 36 cm (14¼ in.). *Photo by Tom Mills.*

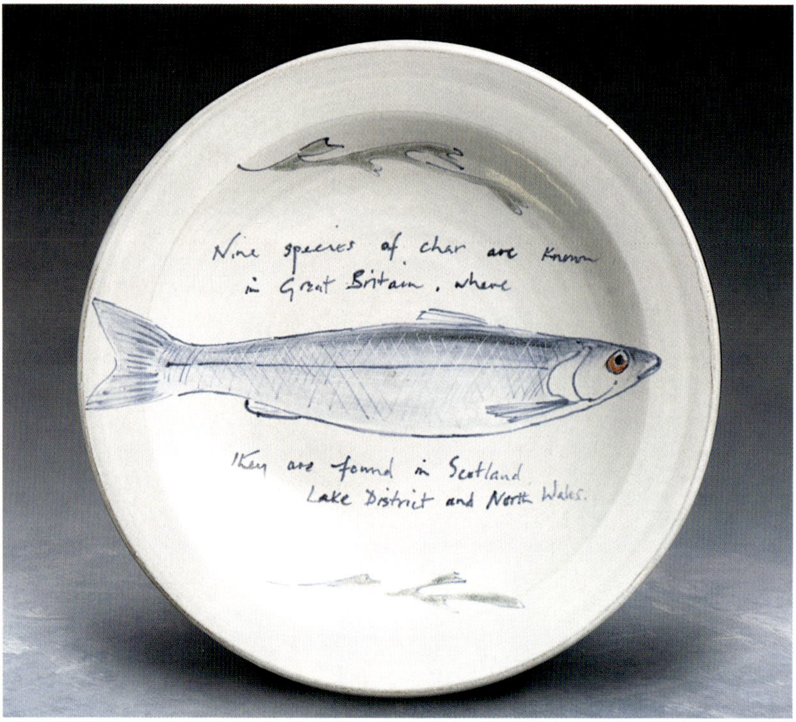

Char, shallow dish by Molly Attrill. Dia: 29 cm (11½ in.). Text taken from an early 20th century natural history encyclopaedia. There is a long tradition of inscriptions on tin glaze. *Photo by Steve Thearle.*

Molly Attrill describes her work as 'understated' or 'quiet', as she feels that these are features of her best work. Her love of drawing made maiolica a natural choice of medium. She works with a sanded red body (Swanblend supplied by Clayman of Chichester), and her pieces are either thrown or press-moulded. After biscuit firing, she uses a lead-boron based glaze with 10% tin oxide and 2% zinc oxide, a recipe designed by Alan Caiger-Smith – biscuit firing to cone 07 and glaze firing to cone 04–03. For colours she uses cobalt, red iron, manganese and copper oxides and prepared pigments.

Of maiolica, she comments that it is '...a particularly challenging medium because it requires bringing so many factors together successfully. Loading the brush appropriately can only be learnt through experience. I'd say that the spontaneity of brushwork on tin glaze usually belies the skills involved, because there is so little margin for error ... '.

Posey Bacopoulos presents a contemporary approach to the traditional maiolica of the Italian Renaissance. In her work, the floral motifs are patterns rather than actual representations. Along with grid designs and dots, they serve to divide the space of the pot in interesting ways. This reveals a strong influence from Japanese Oribe ceramics, as well as from Islamic and

European sources. She uses Stanley Mace Andersen's red clay body to throw, alter and assemble her pieces. Her in-glaze painting is carried out on a matt glaze:

PB Matt Majolica (cone 04)

Ferro Frit 3124	65
EPK	20
Dolomite	10
Flint	5
Zircopax	10

3 tbsp Epsom salts are mixed in solution per 5 gallons (approx. 20 litres) of glaze.

For colourants, a variety of Mason stains, Amaco GDCs (straight from the bottle), and Duncan's Easy Stroke #EZ 12 Black are used. The Mason stains are mixed with Posey's Stain Paste by volume in the ratio of one part Mason stain to 3.5 parts stain paste:

Posey's Stain Paste (mix by volume)

Gerstley borate (UK use calcium borate frit)	1 part
Ferro frit 3124	1 part

Mix with water to a paste-like consistency and strain.

The pots are biscuit fired very slowly to cone 05 so that the gases in the clay burn out. This helps to prevent white-spotting in the finished piece. Then, the pots are dipped into the glaze and allowed to dry over night.

When decorating, Bacopoulos uses various sizes of brushes to apply the colours – working from the foreground to the background so as to always paint on a white ground. In between each layer, she uses wax resist, giving her the freedom to paint over already decorated parts without ruining them. As an example of this, she will paint leaves and then wax, paint flowers and then wax,

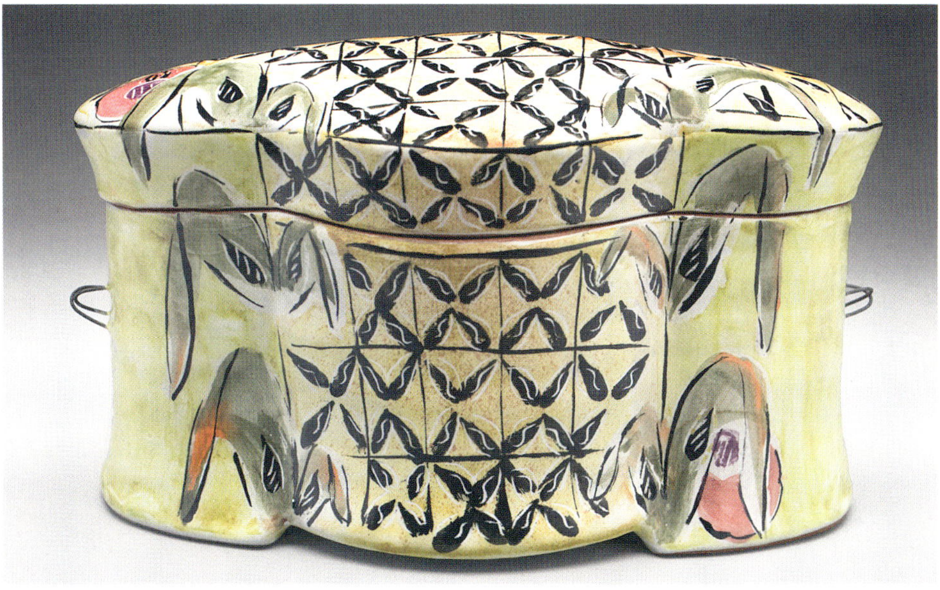

Large oval box by Posey Bacopoulos. 13.5 cm x 27.5 cm x15 cm (5½ x 10¾ x 6 in.). *Photo by Kevin Nobel.*

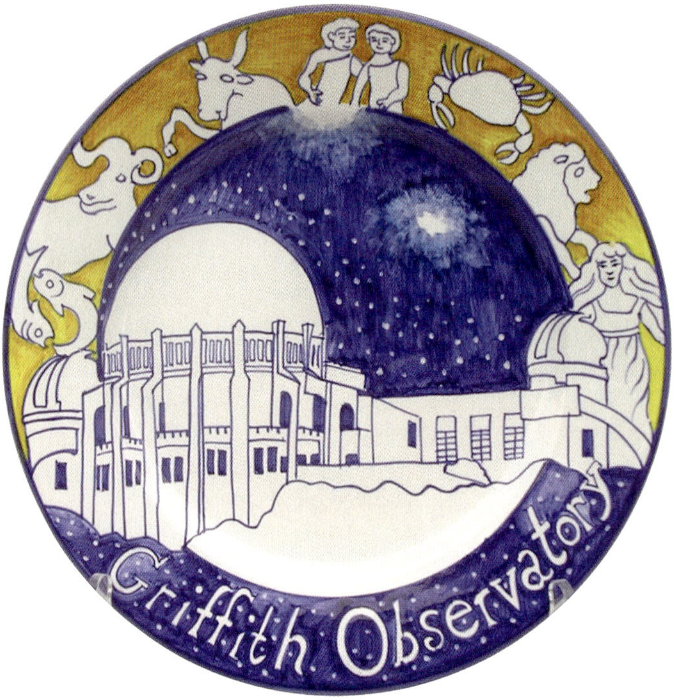

Griffith Observatory plate by Karen Koblitz, 2003. Dia: 25.5 cm (10 in.). *Photo by Susan Einstein.*

and then lastly paint the background.

To add variety to the surface, she uses a mouth atomiser to spray another colour over the background – such as rutile (mixed with stain paste) over yellow. The black lines, grids and dots are then painted at the end, on top of the background. As she decorates, she also sgraffitos through both the black lines and the colour to bring up the white beneath. This adds variety to the lines, and helps define both the space and the shapes. The pots are then fired extremely slowly to cone 04.

Karen Koblitz has been designing dinnerware for the Grazia factory in Deruta, Italy, since 1989, and she uses many of the traditional maiolica techniques learnt there in her own work. The 'Los Angeles Souvenir Plate' series was created during a 2003 summer residency at the factory. The idea for the series came as she was preparing works for a solo show in Russia, in which she wanted to share a bit of her home city of Los Angeles with the Russian audience. The sites selected for the plates are some of Koblitz's favourite places in Los Angeles.

Once bisque-fired to cone 04, the plates were covered with a tin-oxide based white matt glaze (*smalto*). The designs were then transferred to the unfired glaze using the traditional method of 'pouncing' where charcoal is rubbed onto the glaze surface through a series of small holes punched in a paper pattern. The patterns were then outlined and filled in with colourful oxides. A clear glaze (*vetrina*) was sprayed on the ware before the glost firing to cone 07.

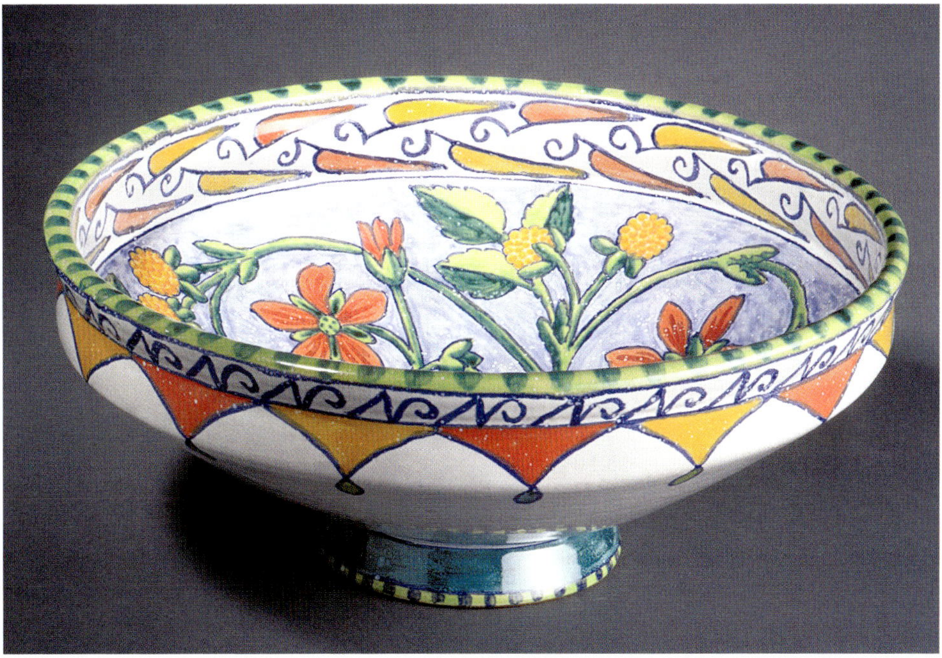

Salmon Berry bowl by Terry Siebert, 2001. 33 × 12.8 cm (13 × 5 in.) *Photo by Roger Schreiber.*

Terry Siebert

I continue to be inspired by the intricacies of nature and the rich traditions of majolica pottery. I love the meditative process of immersing myself in nature and sketching my observations. In the studio, I play with the sketches, allowing historical influences and the pot form to enter into the design process. I admire the exotic form and ornamentation of Persian ceramics with its highly abstracted, imaginative, plant-derived designs. I also enjoy Spanish lustre-ware with its lively, calligraphic brushwork and designs – utilising the interplay of positive and negative space. Ultimately, the process of pottery making is a means of connecting myself to the natural world, other cultures and artists before me, and to those who now find meaning in my work.

Most of Siebert's pottery is thrown. The biscuit firing is to Orton cone 05.

Siebert white majolica glaze
(cone 05)

Ferro Frit #3124	72
Flint	10
EPK (China clay)	12
Zircopax	10
In-glaze pigments	
Frit #3124	75
Stain or oxide	25

Mix with a spoonful of laundry starch or glycerine and water to help prevent smudging and aid flow.

Siebert mostly uses Mason's stains with some Amaco GDCs (for chartreuse green, orange and red).

I paint with good quality sumi brushes, and sometimes watercolour brushes.

Ideally the brush should hold a quantity of glaze and come to a fine point. I paint with the in-glaze pigments as if using watercolours. I like bright, opaque colours, so I am not afraid to put down a thick coat of in-glaze.

Stoneware maiolica

Maiolica techniques can also be used effectively at high temperatures, although the overall look is different due to the greater integration of stoneware glaze and body. Maiolica fired to stoneware temperatures creates more durable, non-porous pieces which avoid common low-fired problems such as crazing and metal release. A comparable colour palette is achieved thanks to the wide spectrum of high-firing stains which are now available. Mohamed Hamid and Laurence McGowan are two practitioners working with stoneware maiolica.

Laurence McGowan uses Scarva's Earthstone Original off-white stoneware body for his thrown and press-moulded pieces. They are then biscuit fired to 960°C (1760°F). In-glaze decoration is carried out with freely applied brushstrokes using oxide and stain mixtures which include a small amount of gum Arabic – essential to get them to flow off the brush. The glaze firing is to 1260°C (2300°F). (See illustration on p.42.)

McGowan's stoneware maiolica glaze (cone 8)

Cornish stone	38
Whiting	13
Dolomite	7
Zinc oxide	1
Ball clay	10
Flint	19
Zirconium silicate	12

Mohamed Hamid, inspired by Islamic and European tin-glazed earthenware, uses a technique known as 'one-stroke' for his brushwork. This uses big, bold strokes and then detailed outlining in black or blue, with some sgraffito work added through the brush strokes. Hamid spent his formative years at Aldermaston Pottery, and there was fortunate to train with Alan Caiger-Smith and Edgar Campden. He uses an iron-free stoneware clay, as darker iron-bearing bodies adversely affect the glaze and discolour the decoration. Biscuit firing is to 1000°C (1832°F). The glaze is a stable opaque white

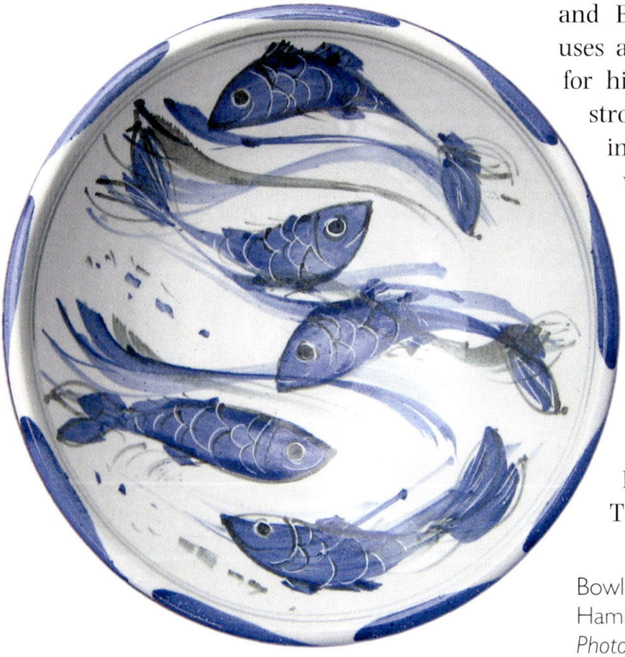

Bowl with blue fish pattern, by Mohamed Hamid. Dia: 33 cm (13 in.), ht: 4 cm (1½ in.). *Photo courtesy of the artist.*

glaze which takes colour well, including chrome. Fired to 1280°C (2336°F), it benefits from a soak at top temperature.

Hamid's stoneware maiolica glaze
(cone 10)

Cornish stone	17
Potash feldspar	21
Whiting	9
Dolomite	8.8
China clay	13.5
Hyplas	1.5
Flint	28.5
Zirconium silicate	12

Blue pigment

Cobalt carbonate	40
Red iron oxide	10
China clay	20
Hyplas ball clay	20
Feldspar	13

Add water and grind for 1 hour

Sgraffito

This is the process of scratching through one layer to reveal another contrasting one underneath. Usually, it is done through a layer of strong, dark colour to the glaze, producing a white line which has the effect of highlighting or defining features of a design. It can also, however, be done through wax prior to the inlaying of a pigment (see William Newland's use of this technique p.72).

Fine sgraffito lines can be made using a needle or pointed bamboo tool. For thicker lines, Matthias Ostermann recommends using the tip of a plastic spoon. Whatever the tool, the pressure must be light and flowing – otherwise, it is easy to go right through to the body and chip the raw glaze. William Newland often used a technique of sgraffito through wax (see p.72).

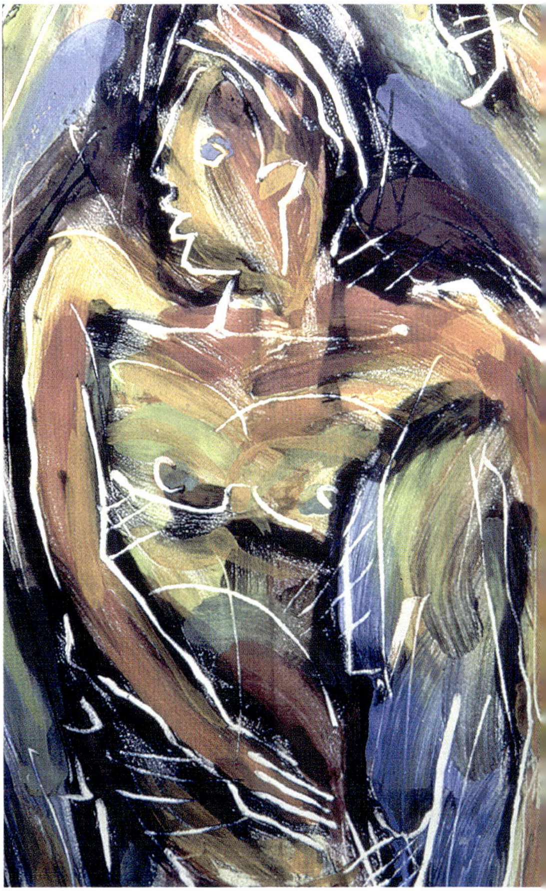

Heron vase by Matthias Ostermann, detail, 2000. Ht: 62 cm (24½ in.). (See also *Icarus plate* p.52). *Photo by Jan Thujs. Courtesy of Daniel Grummisch.*

Hennie Meyer
Meyer's work reflects the development of several basic forms with particular emphasis on design elements and decoration. He especially enjoys working with composite shapes such as jugs and teapots. Meyer slabs and press-moulds his forms using a high-firing red earthenware body, biscuit firing to 980°C (1796°F) and glaze firing to 1196°C (2185°F). When using lustres, these are fired to 780°C (1436°F).

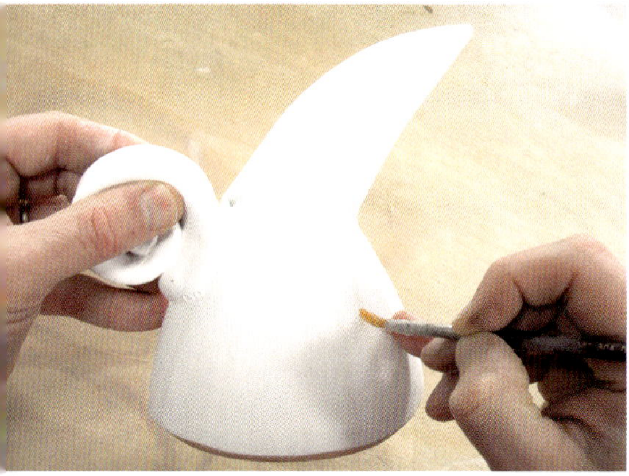

1 Hennie Meyer applying cold wax to a glazed jug.

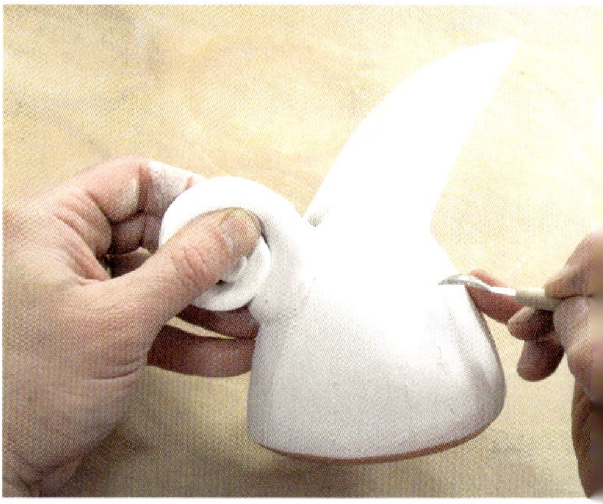

2. Sgraffito through wax to glaze.

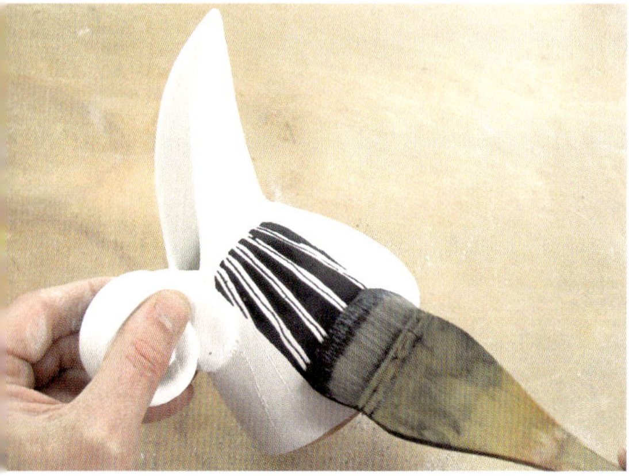

3. Applying cobalt oxide over waxed and sgraffitoed glaze surface.

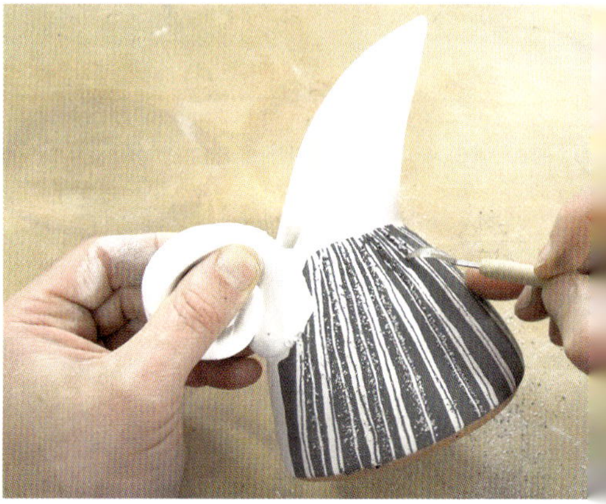

4 Completing design with sgraffito lines through oxide revealing glaze underneath.

Meyer's glaze recipe (cone 5)	
Lead bisilicate	50
Frit FSB510	10
Cornish stone	30
Whiting	3
Kaolin GI	11
Tin oxide	11
Bentonite	2

Designs are painted in various oxide mixtures of blues and blacks, and sgraffito marks represent a strong element of the decoration (see oxide mixtures chart, p.35).

Sponging, sponge printing and stencils

The sponging of pigment onto tin glaze is a device that was commonly used in English Delftware – either as a background filler or to represent foliage. Sponges can also be used with stencils and cut into shapes for printing. Hylton Nel and Bronwyn Williams-Ellis both use sponging techniques in their work. (For use of stencils with slips under tin glaze, please see the work of Morgen Hall, p.88.)

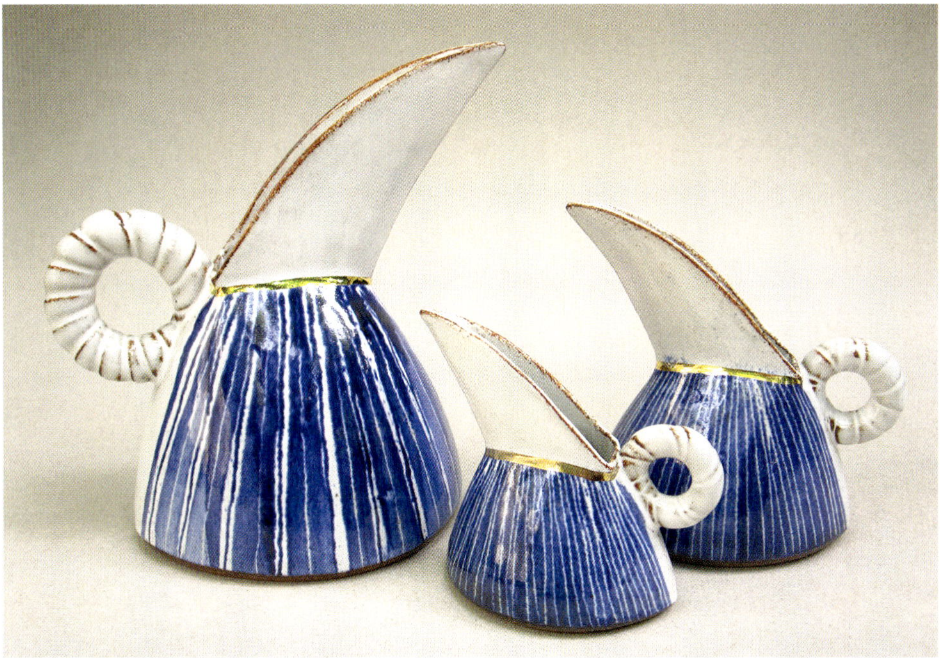

Group of fired jugs by Hennie Meyer, max. ht: 15.5 cm (6 in.), 2010. *Photos by Alessandro Pappada.*

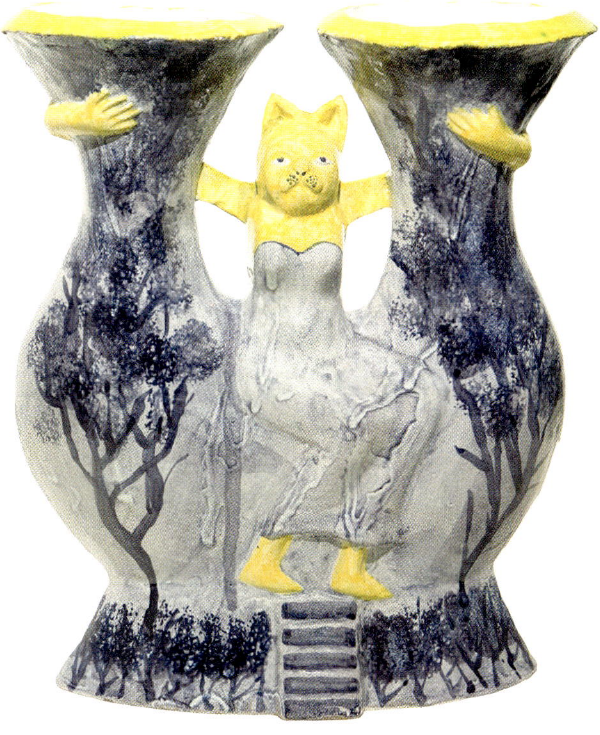

Cat lady, double vase by Hylton Nel, 2009. Ht: 29.5 cm (11¾in.), w: 25 cm (10 in.). As well as the painted line, Nel makes liberal use of sponging, usually with cobalt or manganese oxides. *Courtesy of Michael Stevenson, Cape Town.*

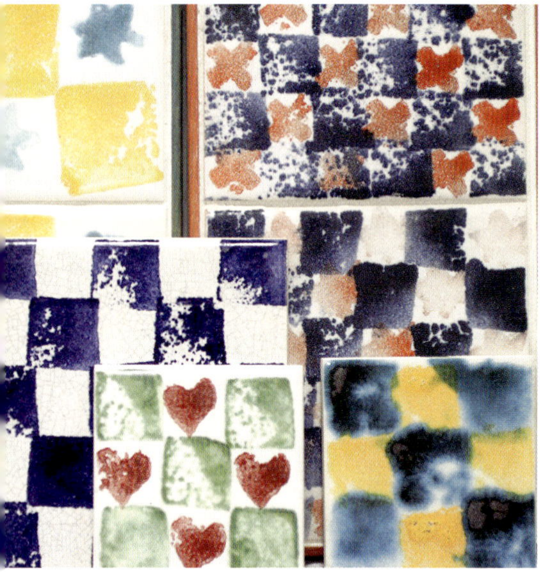

Sponge-printed tiles by Bronwyn Williams-Ellis. Shaped sponges are hand-cut with a zscalpel. Stains and oxides are sieved dry through 200 mesh sieve to combine, before printing on top of unfired alkaline tin glaze surface. *Photo courtesy of the artist.*

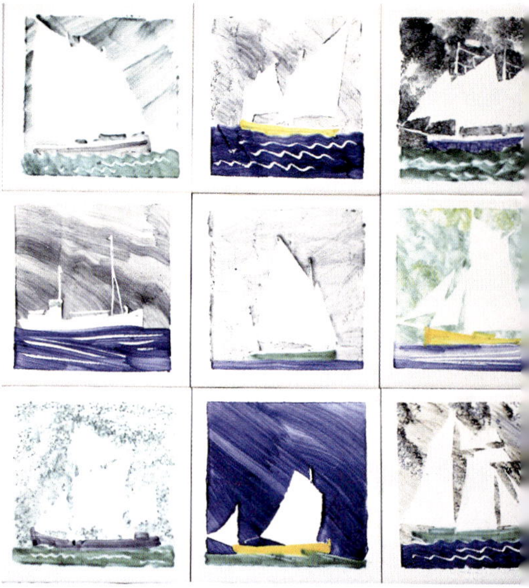

Traditional Boats tile panel, by Bronwyn Williams-Ellis. Standard 15.3 x 15.3 cm (6 x 6 in.) tiles. Stencils are cut from heavy duty 'builder's' thickness polythene. The tiles are glazed with a white, matt, alkaline tin glaze, and the background consists of cobalt, copper, nickel, manganese and yellow stain mixes – either sponged or brushed over the stencils. *Photo courtesy of the artist.*

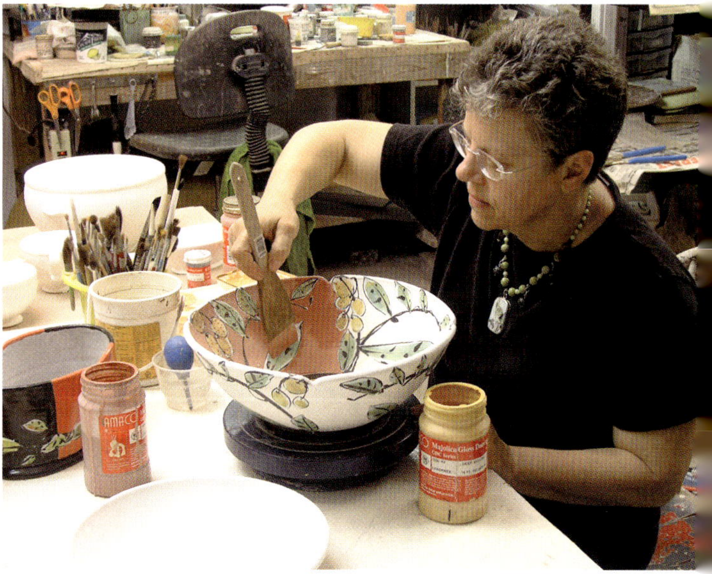

Linda Arbuckle painting background colour over wax resisted areas on a large bowl. *Photo courtesy of the artist.*

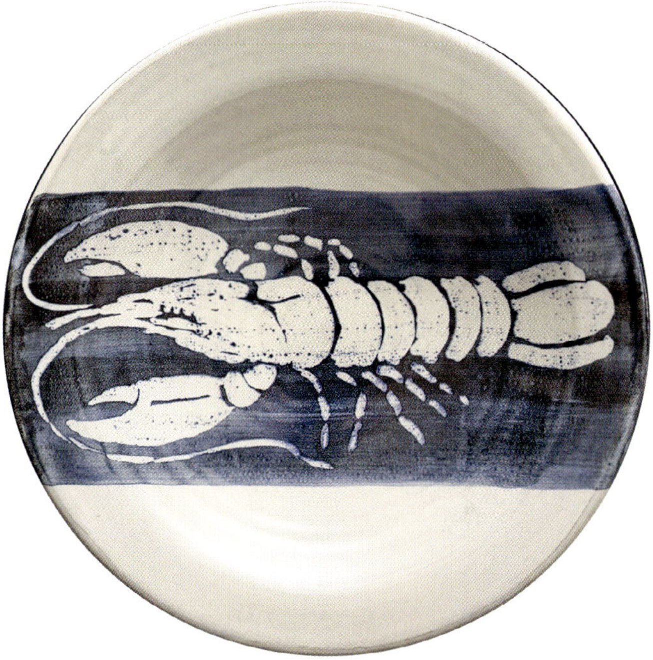

Lobster shallow dish, by Molly Attrill. Dia: 34 cm (13½ in.). Wax resist and cobalt wash. *Photo by Steve Thearle.*

Wax resist, *cuerda seca*

Wax resist has many applications in maiolica, masking body, glaze or colour to create a variety of effects. There are advantages to both hot and cold wax: hot wax (for details see p.26) hardens immediately and resists very effectively, but requires dedicated brushes which have a relatively short life; cold wax emulsion is easy to use and does not require special brushes, but takes longer to dry and does not resist so effectively.

In its simplest form, wax is often used to mask off decorated areas so that a background colour can be evenly painted across the whole surface.

Posey Bacopoulos (see p.60) uses wax in between each layer of colour, which allows her the freedom to paint over the already decorated parts without ruining them.

Wax resist can also be used as a painting medium in itself, as in the work of Molly Attrill and Kate Scott. Both use wax to paint their designs and the waxed areas then resist the cobalt oxide wash which is painted on top. Attrill describes her technique:

> I have worked to refine my decorating technique for years, and the series of dishes with wax resist was an attempt to give the timeless qualities of tin-glaze ware a contemporary simplicity. I have always been attracted to blue and white traditions, and I love the 'soft/silkiness' of old delft wares. With the wax resist designs, everything depends on the quality of the cobalt wash, the richness of the blue and the serendipitous residues of the wash bubbling and gathering on the waxed areas. I was, of course, seeking to give the effect of a single wash, but it required several sweeps of a wide, flat brush, using different strengths of the wash which is a mix of cobalt oxide, red iron oxide and manganese – I confess done by eye rather than meticulous measurement.

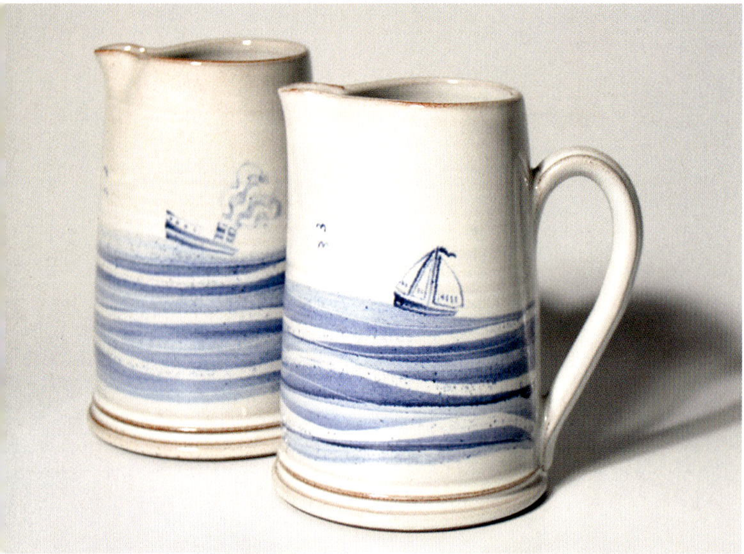

Boat jugs by Kate Scott. Ht: 11.5 cm (4½ in.). Cobalt wash over wax resist. *Photo courtesy of the artist.*

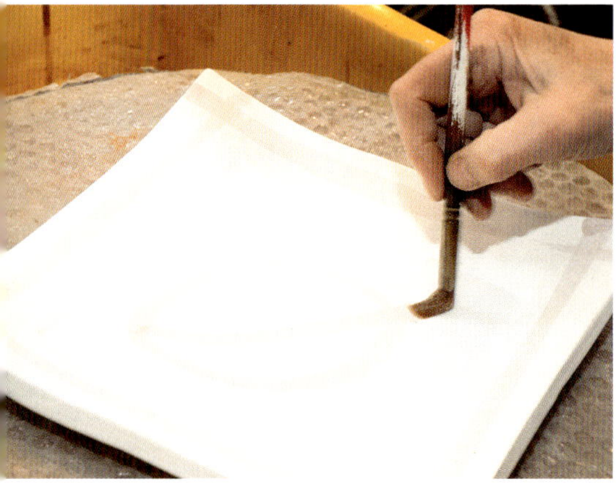

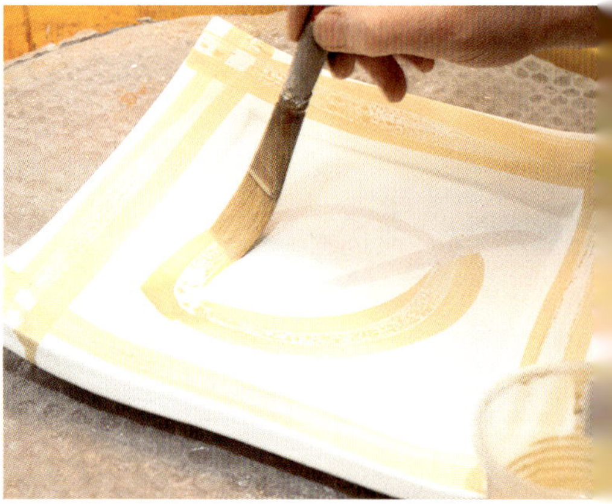

ABOVE Painting wax on to glaze.

ABOVE RIGHT Painting first colour – soft yellow – over wax.

RIGHT Wax has been painted over the yellow and the second colour – rust – is brushed on.

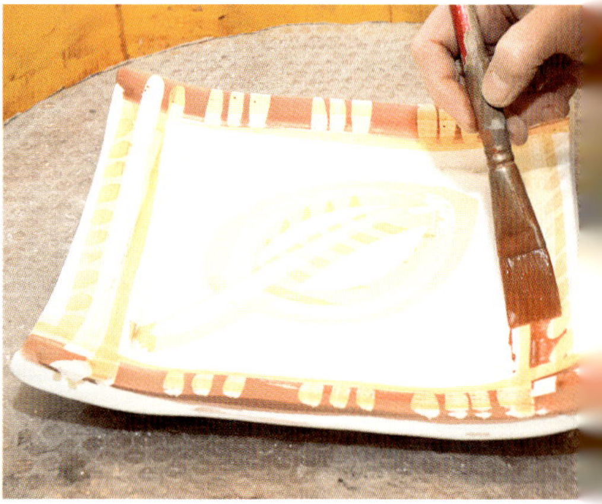

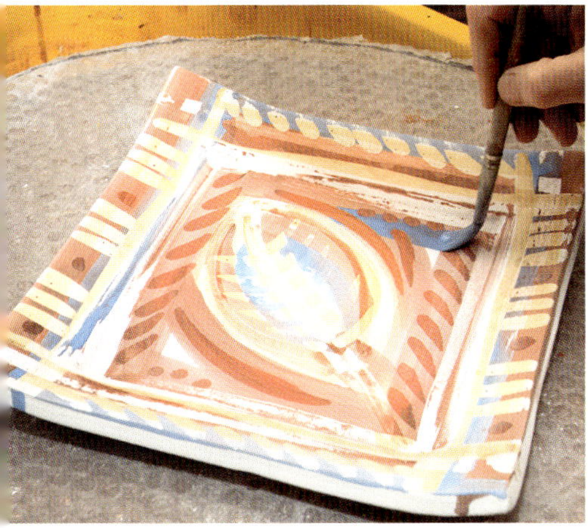

Further wax painting has been added over the rust areas and the third colour – light blue – is now applied.

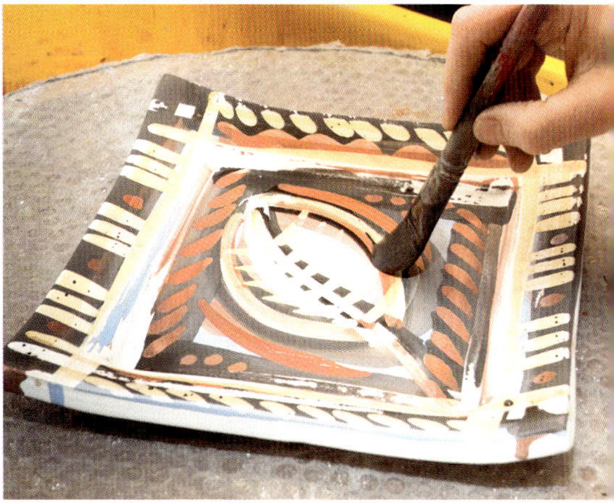

After final wax application, a strong blue-black is the last colour to be added.

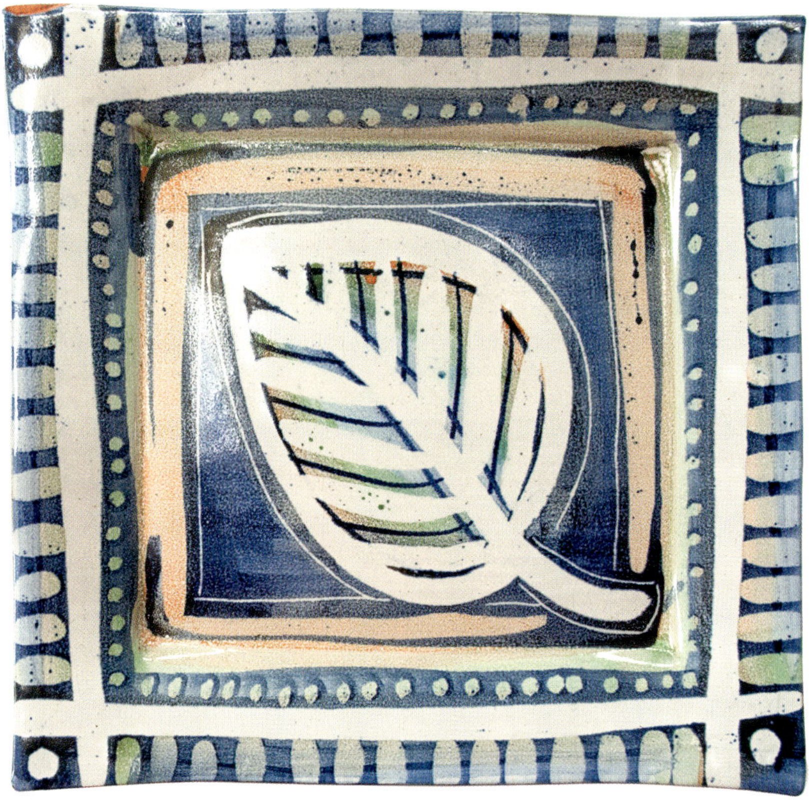

Multi-layered wax-resist square dish by Daphne Carnegy. 26 × 26 cm (10¼ × 10¼ in.). *Photos by Naomi Schillinger.*

A rich, coloured, layered effect can be created by multi-layering wax and pigments – firstly using wax resist directly on the raw glaze, and then painting on alternate areas of colour and wax. With this method, it is best to start with paler colours and then work up to darker ones.

A technique much used by **William Newland** starts with a design etched into wax-coated leatherhard clay. A black glaze suitable for raw firing is then applied to the etched areas. After the piece has been biscuit fired, a white tin glaze is applied to the whole surface. In-glaze pigments can be applied at this stage, often (in Newland's case) in combination with wax resist. In the subsequent glaze firing, the black glaze burns through the tin glaze to give a soft manganese brown outline.

Newland's black glaze (cone 03)

Lead bisilicate	75
Ball clay	25
Manganese dioxide	10

Cuerda seca ('dry cord' in Spanish) is a technique first developed in Hispano-Moresque tin-glazed ware, and is a ceramic version of batik. Wax is stained with colouring oxide, usually manganese dioxide, and the outline of the design is painted or trailed on to the biscuit-fired surface. These areas resist the glaze, fire to matt black lines, and serve as barriers between areas of different coloured tin glazes.

Bronwyn Williams-Ellis specialises in hand-made tiles and uses a variety of maiolica techniques – including cuerda seca. She uses wax melted with manganese dioxide applied with a

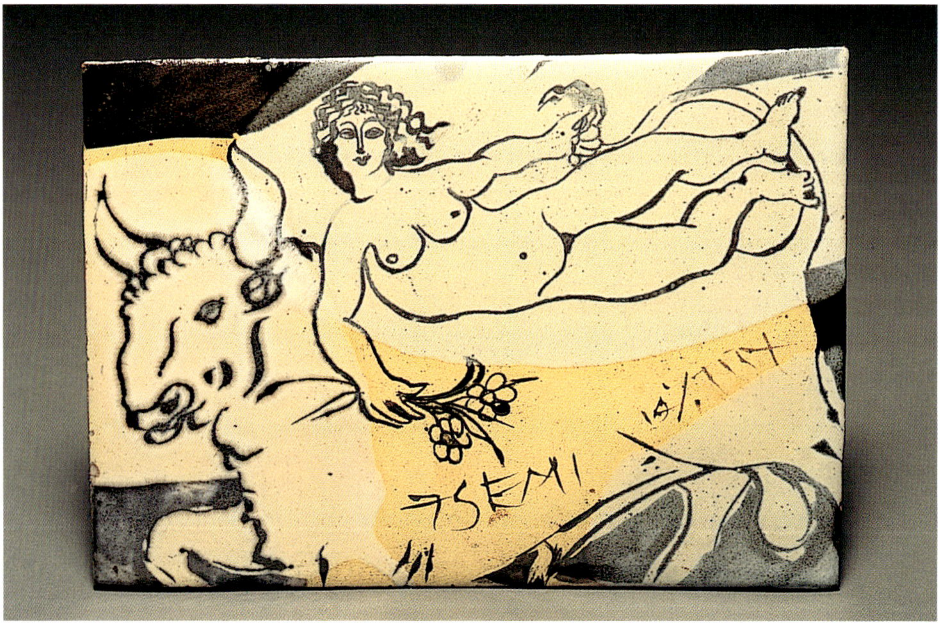

William Newland, test showing use of black glaze inlaid into etched wax line, under tin glaze. *Photo by Douglas Cape.*

Crouched man tile panel, by Bronwyn Williams-Ellis. 46 x 46 cm (18 x 18 in.). Cuerda seca outlines, zirconium-tin white glaze and coloured glazes stained with varied mixes of grey stains. Fired to 1020°C (1868°F). *Photo courtesy of the artist.*

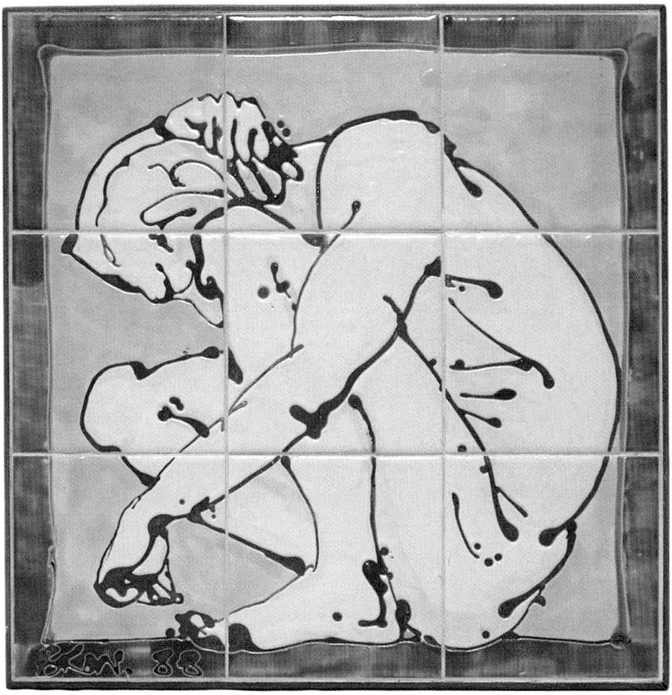

traditional 'Tjanting' batik tool to create the outlines of her design on to the biscuit-fired surface. Tin or zirconium-white and coloured glazes are then applied with a brush between or over the wax resist lines. In the glaze firing, the wax burns off to leave a dry, brown-black outline.

Glaze on glaze

Traditionally, tin glazes have often been tinted, coloured and superimposed. The earliest instance of this practice can be found in Florentine oak-leaf ware (see p.12), where a rich, dark blue glaze is applied over the white tin glaze. Later examples include the *bianco sopra bianco* (white on off-white), the *berretino* (lavender blue) and the *bleu de Nevers* (white on dark blue – revisited in the Delftware of Bristol). The effect of glaze on glaze is different from in-glaze pigment decoration in that, being more viscous and substantial, it creates a slight relief over the base glaze and also has a more glossy appearance.

Farraday Newsome

My work differs from traditional maiolica technique in that I brush multiple layers of coloured glazes onto the white ground glaze, as opposed to washes. My work generally refers to ideas of time, fertility, chance and danger by use of natural and artificial imagery. Usually this imagery is composed in a drift, with associations being made in a personal and fluid manner. I have been most influenced by my childhood in the forest, where nature in both its darkest and lightest manifestations surrounded me. As

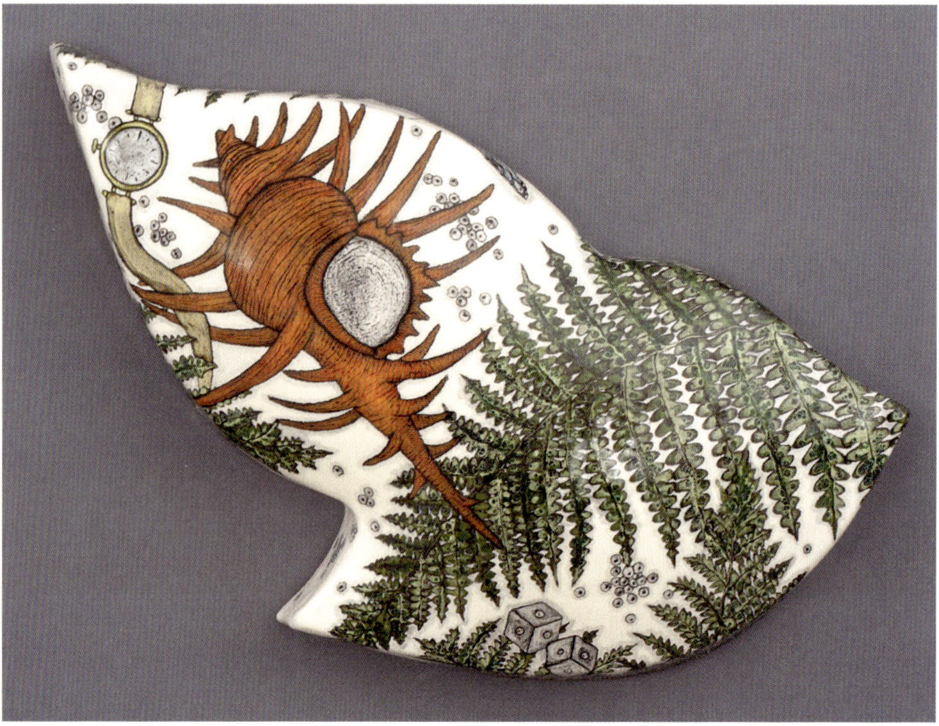

Fern and Shell Cloud Fragment, by Farraday Newsome, 2008. 48.2 x 35.6 x 7.6 cm (19 x 14 x 3 in.). Maiolica with coloured glazes.

'This is a remembrance of my childhood in the ferns of the California redwood forest, near the beautiful Pacific ocean with its tidepools and shells. This piece hangs on the wall, its shape that of a formed canvas with an undulating surface.' *Photo courtesy of the artist.*

an adult, I have been influenced by the cool, precise paintings of the Northern Renaissance, by the starker studio still-life paintings of mid-20th century American painters Edwin Dickinson and Adolph Gottleib, and by the contemporary, painterly ceramics of Michael Lucero and Paul Mathieu. I am also influenced by the painterly work and keen insights of my ceramicist husband Jeff Reich.

Newsome uses a grogged red terracotta for the hand-built wall tiles, using soft slabs to form the curving walls. Bisque temperature is to cone 1.

White maiolica glaze (Andrea Gill's) (cone 05)

Ferro frit 3124	100
Colemanite/Gerstley Borate/Borax frit	4
EPK China clay	15
Zircopax (20%)	24
Bentonite (2%)	3

The coloured glazes that Newsome uses to paint her imagery are either the standard white glaze (with 8% glaze stains giving creamy opaque glazes), or the same glaze without the zircopax (giving a clear, semi-transparent glaze). She also buys ready-made cone 05 glazes from a variety of manufacturers for an even greater range of colours.

After bisque firing, the white glaze is sprayed onto the work. It is then sinter fired (to cone 014) to set the glaze into a tough matt ground. Next, the design is sketched onto the sintered white surface with soft vine charcoal before layers of glaze colours are brushed on. The work is then glaze fired to cone 05.

Bianco sopra bianco

This was a subtle decorative effect originally developed in Faenza in the High Renaissance. It was taken up later in English Delftware, where it was mostly used on rims and borders. It consists of the use of warm, off-white base glaze sometimes tinted with manganese, over which decoration is applied in a cooler white tin glaze.

'Black' maiolica

The technique of 'black' maiolica is variously used, but basically involves the use of maiolica glazes and pigments over a black base glaze, often with wax resist. This creates a very different effect from traditional maiolica. The black glaze is revealed in parts, and also burns through and affects the maiolica glaze and in-glaze colours.

Walter Ostrom has been using a similar glaze-on-glaze technique for the past few years, which he calls 'neo-maiolica'. The base glaze is his usual maiolica glaze, but substituting 10% black stain for the zirconium silicate opacifier. The design is drawn on the black glaze with trailed wax, and then the entire piece is dipped into the white maiolica glaze. In-glaze colours, including soluble salts, stains

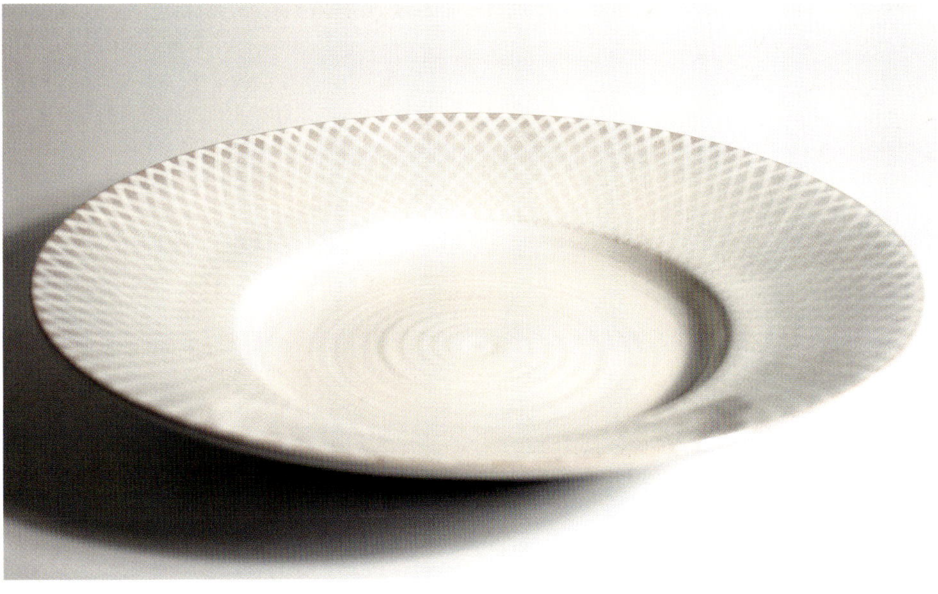

Bianco sopra bianco dish by Kate Scott. Dia: 36 cm (14¼ in.). The '*bianco*' is the same glaze with extra tin oxide, applied with a brush to the raw (thinly) glazed surface. Crawling can be a problem if it is applied too thickly. *Photo courtesy of the artist.*

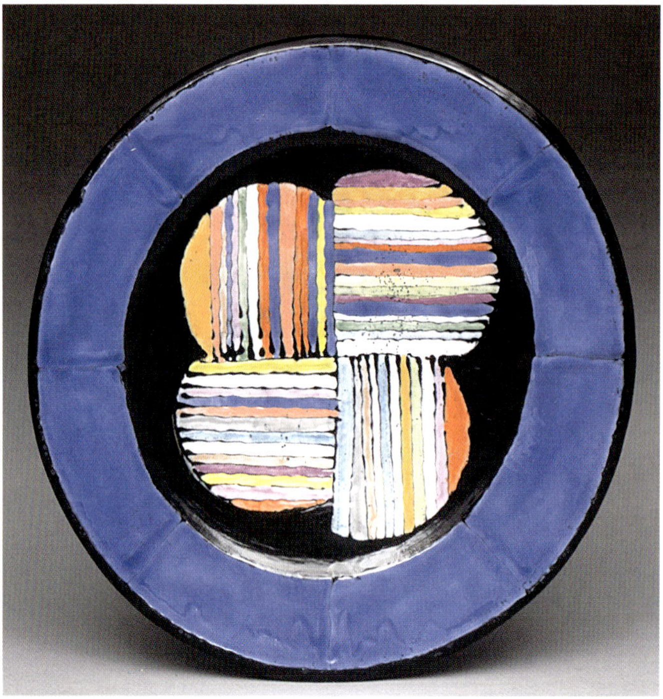

Neo-maiolica plate by Walter Ostrom. Dia: 32 cm (12½ in.). *Photo by Julian Beveridge Photographic.*

with frit, commercial maiolica colours and home-made glazes, are then applied on top of the glaze. Firing is to cone 04–05 with a 30–40 minute soak.

Walter Ostrom's Sweet White
(cone 04–05)

Ferro frit 3292	32
Ferro frit 3124	34
Zircopax	12
EPK china clay	8
Whiting	5
Kona F-4 feldspar	5
Nepheline syenite	2
Flint	2
Bentonite	1

Susannah Lints describes her technique:

Black maiolica is a balance between the thickness and viscosity of the black layer and the thickness and viscosity of the white layer. It is a constant dance, and it is an art, not a science! How thickly we apply this glaze will also affect the outcome. When the black layer is heavier, then more breaking and black spots appear. You can reduce this effect by making the layers equal. It is a 5-step process.

She outlines her procedure:

- Apply black maiolica base and let dry
- Apply design with wax emulsion and allow to dry overnight
- Apply thin layer of white maiolica – adding two teaspoons of CMC gum solution per pint allows this to be applied with a brush
- Apply pigments

Beakers by Susannah Lints, black maiolica, ht: 17.8 cm (7 in.). *Photo by Courtney Frisse.*

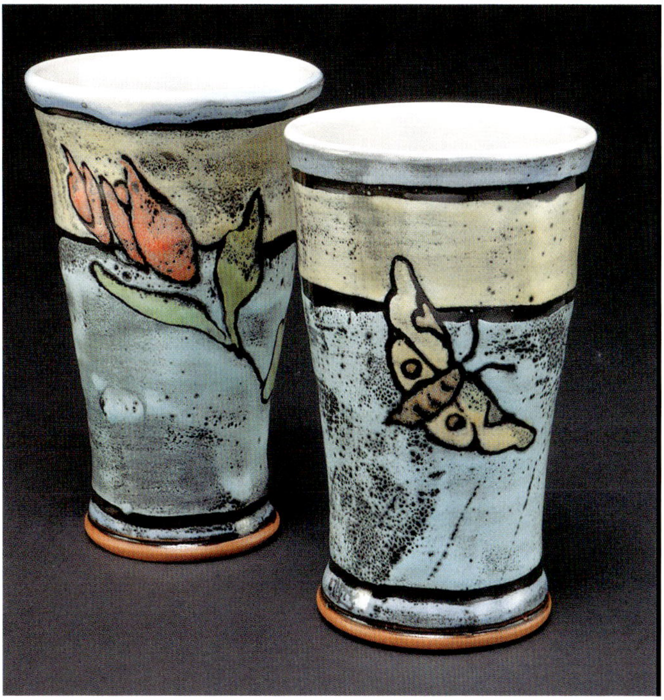

- Fire at medium speed to cone 05

Two of her glaze recipes are given here. For the black base, omit the zirconium and tin oxides and instead add 10–12% Mason stain 6600.

Linda Arbuckle's (cone 05)

Ferro frit 3124	58
F-4 feldspar (unispar)	20
EPK kaolin	2
Nepheline Syenite	7
Zircopax	10
Tin	5
Bentonite	2

Nina's 04 (cone 04)

Ferro frit 3124	66
F-4 feldspar (unispar)	18
EPK Kaolin	10
Nepheline syenite	6
Zircopax	14
Bentonite	2

Terry Siebert works with a different process for her black maiolica – she paints the pigments directly on a black glaze in the same manner as she would on a traditional white glaze. There is no layering of glazes as in the work of Ostrom and Lints. The in-glaze decoration interacts with the black base in different and interesting ways: copper oxide, for example, looks almost iridescent on top of the black.

Black Majolica Glaze (cone 05)

Ferro frit #3124	72
Flint (silica)	10
Edgar plastic kaolin	12
Mason stain # 6650	8

(a cobalt-free black stain – otherwise glaze will have a bluish color)

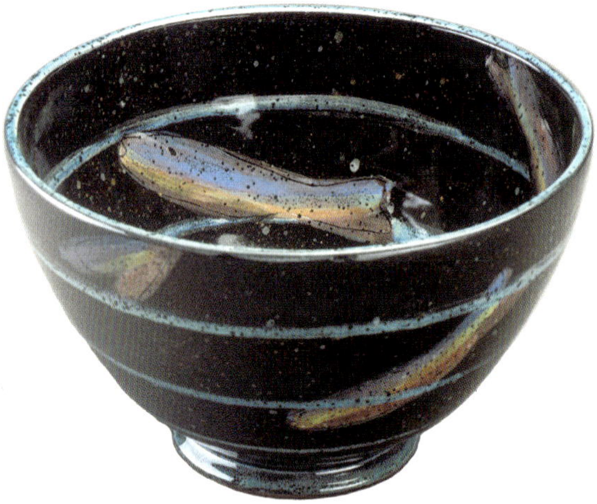

Fish bowl by Terry Siebert. 17.8 × 20.3 cm (7 × 8 in.). Black maiolica. *Photo by Roger Schreiber.*

On-glaze decoration: decals, lustres, enamels

Decals

These are transfers used to place a ceramic pigment or enamel design on to the ceramic surface. They are applied on to the surface of the fired maiolica glaze, which may already have been decorated with in-glaze painting, and can provide an added layer of interest or definition to the overall design. In the cases of Philip Eglin and Kari Radasch which follow, they serve to recreate a drawn line (in contrast to a painted line).

Decals can be made using either ceramic pigments (ie. oxides or stains) or enamels. The main difference between the two being that decals made only with pigments need to be fired up to a high enough temperature for the oxide or stain to be well assimilated into the underlying fired glaze – usually at least 1000°C (1832°F). In contrast, enamel decals (which can be thought of as very low-fired glazes) are only fired up to a temperature sufficient for the glaze to soften slightly and bond with the enamel – typically in the range 780–840°C (1436–1544°F). Enamel decals have a very different look from the pigment transfers, remaining as a distinct and tactile layer on top of the maiolica glaze surface. Companies specialising in making decals from original artwork can be found either on the internet, or in ceramic journals. Computer-scanned drawings can also be laser-printed on to coated water-slide decal paper.

Philip Eglin's work abounds with historical references, and tin glaze is both an ideal source and a vehicle for these post-modern reworkings. In the plate illustrated, a Cranach-sourced image is framed by borders in an iconic early Italianate palette of copper and manganese. The plate is press-moulded in white earthenware and then crimped by hand while soft. A high bisque firing to 1140°C (2084°F) is followed by application of tin glaze, and copper carbonate and manganese dioxide in-glaze painting. After glost firing to 1060°C (1940°F), the cobalt carbonate decal of the *Three Graces* drawing is applied and the plate is fired again to 1060°C.

Kari Radasch, a self-confessed admirer of cakes, applies appliqué slab motifs to her pieces rather as a baker applies fondant icing to a cake! Maiolica glaze is used, unconventionally, for its 'stiff and marshmallowy' texture, as a raised

Three Graces plate by Philip Eglin, 2007. Dia: 22 cm (8¾ in.). *Collection of the author.*

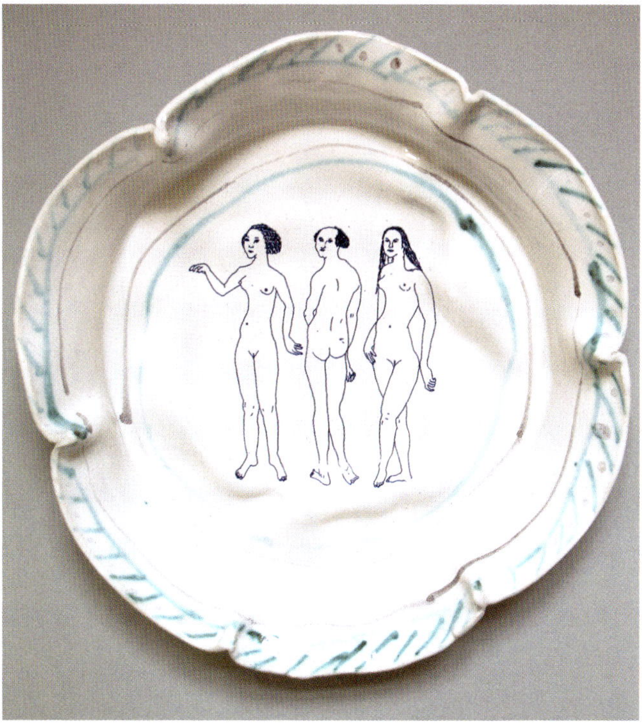

BELOW *Applique* serving dish, by Kari Radasch, 2009. W: 23 cm (9 in.). Terracotta, coloured glazes, white maiolica glaze, iron transfer decals. *Photo courtesy of the artist.*

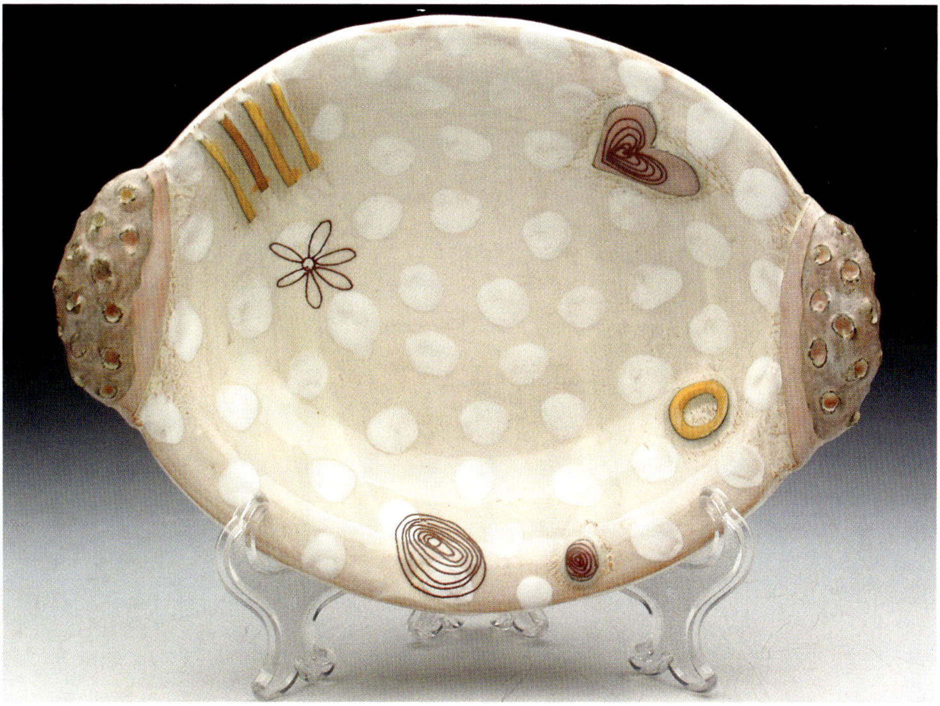

surface floating on top of clear coloured glazes, and in combination with on-glaze iron transfer decals.

> One can build it up or carve it away. I also love that it will stay put no matter how thick it is. The thick, white, frosty finger painted spots are an example of how I use majolica to 'float' on top of the coloured glazes. The glaze firing is to cone 03. The final layer is a hand drawn iron transfer decal which is made using the laser transfer method: I scan my line drawings into the computer and then print them on to pre-covercoated water-slide decal paper. These decals are fired to cone 08.

Reduced-pigment lustres

The use of lustres on fired tin glaze dates right back to 9th century Mesopotamia, where the technique was developed from lustres previously used on glass. It reached its pinnacle in the magnificent Hispano-Moresque wares (see photo, top of p.13). A technically challenging process with a variable success rate, the subtle qualities of the reduced lustres are, when successful, greatly superior to the relatively flat and predictable effects produced by commercial, oxidised lustres.

Practitioners in this field are rare, and **Alan Caiger-Smith** is not only a highly skilled practitioner of the technique, but also a universally acknowledged authority on the subject. Reduced lustres are applied to the fired maiolica glaze and necessitate a third firing in reduction atmosphere, i.e. in a wood, gas or oil-fired kiln where oxygen input can be controlled. Compounds of silver and copper are mixed with a carrier, red ochre, and are applied rather like a slip to the fired glaze surface. Encountering no resistance, brushwork can be more fluid and extended on this surface.

Firing temperature is 660–670°C (1220–1238°F). After firing, the red ochre is rubbed off to reveal the lustres, which result from the reduction of the pigments to the state of pure metals. For more information on the subject, please refer to Caiger-Smith's book *Lustre Pottery.*

Oxidised metallic lustres

A wide variety of metallic and coloured lustres is available from suppliers – gold, platinum, copper, mother-of-pearl, bronze and coloured translucent lustres such as blue, red, orange etc. These are ready to use, although some might need to be diluted with proprietary lustre thinners. The lustres are applied with a soft brush, but pens are now also available. Firing temperature is normally in the range 740–850°C/1364–1562°F), but check the manufacturer's specifications. Aesthetically speaking, lustres need to be used with caution; careful planning is needed with regard to how they will work visually with any in-glaze decoration.

On-glaze enamels

These are very low-firing, opaque coloured glazes which are applied to the fired glaze. They are then fired in a third firing to 780–840°C (1436–1544°F). On-glaze enamels can either be bought in ready-to-use form, or as powders to be mixed with an oil or water-based china paint medium. Method of application is usually with soft brushes. Several firings may be necessary to build up layers or washes of colours.

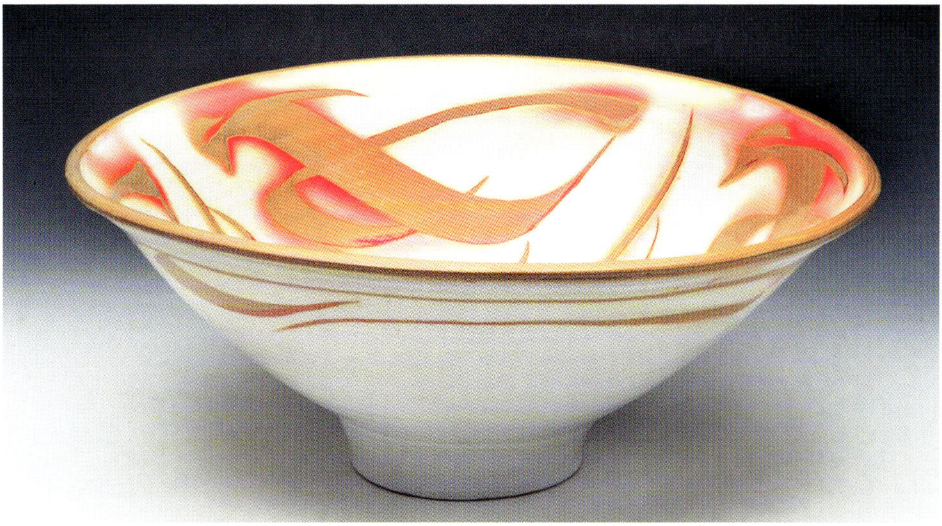

Large tin glaze bowl, by Alan Caiger-Smith, 2006. Dia: 44 cm (17¼ in.), ht: 16 cm (6 in.). Silver-copper reduction lustre with vapour effects. *Photo by Howell Lambert.*

Phyllis Kloda creates intricately constructed and painted narrative vessels and sculptural pieces – decorated with in-glaze maiolica, laser transfers, china paints, decals and gold lustre.

> I find it challenging and fascinating to create a three-dimensional object, and then to activate the surface with an account or tale. The emphasis for this work lies in the construction of elaborate, embellished surfaces reflecting the pots and silverware of the baroque and rococo craftspeople. When designing these, I keep in mind the elements that are important to me, which are beauty, a story or narrative, adornment and colour. I am fascinated with creating small descriptive environments on a three-dimensional surface through which the viewer can explore and discover their own interpretations.

Kloda uses both red and white earthenware bodies, and her construction methods are often combinations of handbuilding, throwing and slipcasting. Biscuit firing is to cone 04. The maiolica glaze is initially fired to cone 018 to set the glaze surface slightly, which makes for an easier surface on which to paint maiolica colourants. The glaze is then fired to its maturing temperature of cone 05–04. Laser transfers are applied to the glaze after the glaze firing, and are then re-fired to cone 05–04. China paints, decals and gold lustre are then added and fired to cone 018.

The in-glaze maiolica colours are Mason stains, mixed in the ratio of one tablespoon of stain to five tablespoons of water. To this is also added a capful of glycerine or Sta-Flo, as this allows the colourants to flow smoothly off the brush.

The china paints are mixed in the traditional manner, combining the dry pigment with various ingredients such as fat oil, lavender, copaiba and clove oils. Using a palette knife and a frosted, flat piece of glass, the dry pigment is mixed with the oils on the glass surface until it has the consistency of toothpaste. The use

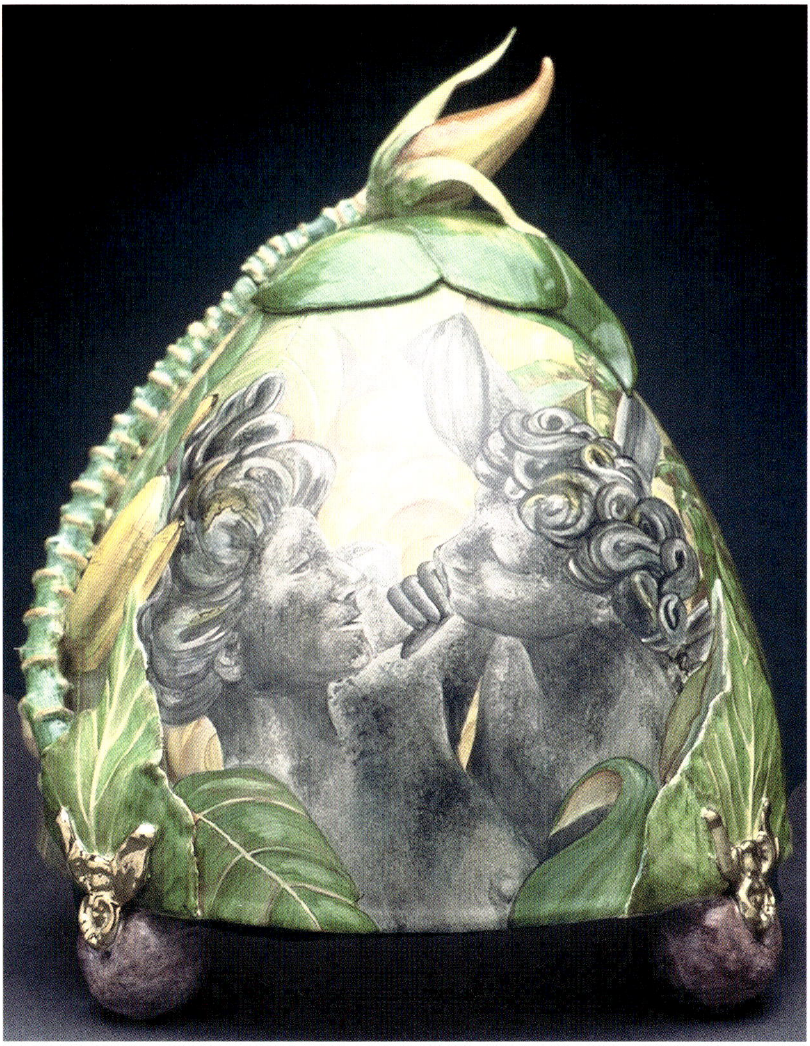

Places That Belong to You by Phyllis Kloda. 54.5 x 35.5 x 35.5 cm (21½ x 14 x 14 in.). White earthenware, maiolica glaze, china paints, lustres. *Photo courtesy of the artist.*

of china paint on maiolica allows for a crisper, more detailed patterning than in-glaze painting is usually able to provide.

Liz Quackenbush uses both lustres and enamels on her richly decorated pieces. Through her work, she aims to create a bridge between the studied elegance of fine china and the robust, utilitarian simplicity of vernacular pottery. She wants to invite use, whilst at the same time seeking to subvert 'run of the mill' pre-conceptions of what functional pottery can or should be. The use of lustres to create a mood of luxury and refinement is in distinct contrast to her use of intentionally retained clay textures and brush marks.

Places That Belong to You, detail. *Photo courtesy of the artist.*

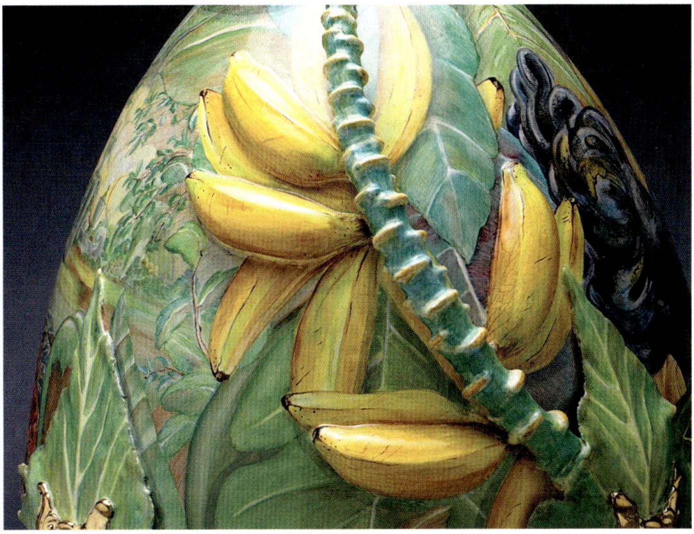

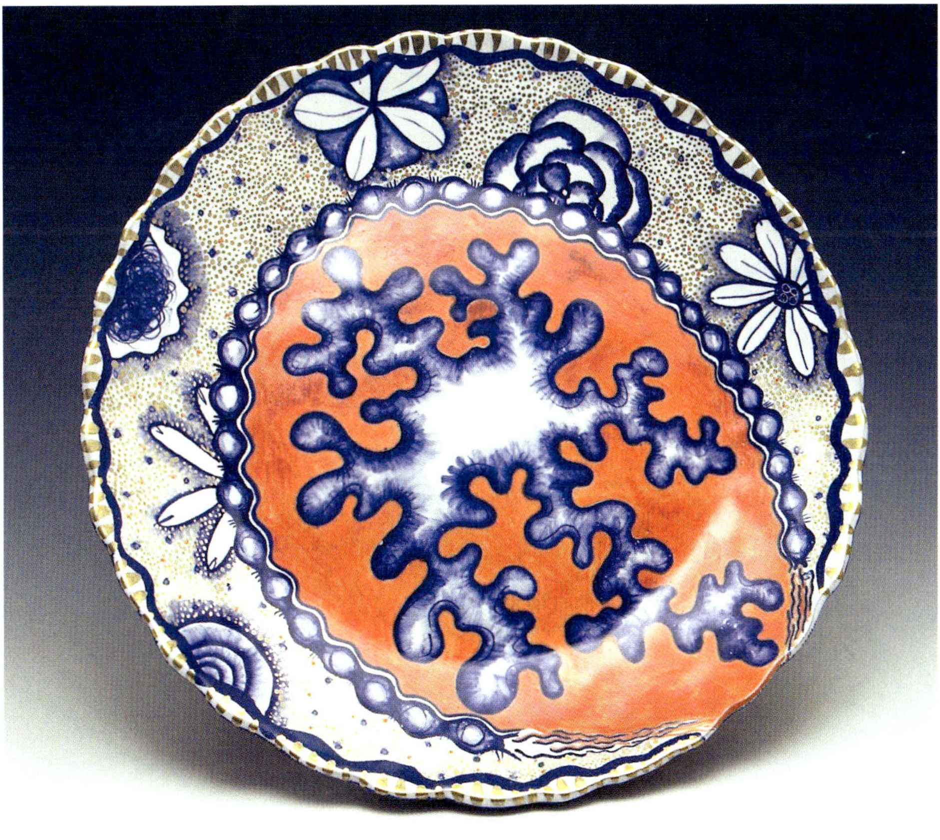

Blob Orange by Liz Quackenbush, 2006. Dia: 45 cm (17¾ in.). Terracotta, maiolica with in-glaze cobalt, lustre, glass enamel. *Photo courtesy of the artist.*

Quackenbush uses terracotta, maiolica with in-glaze pigments, burnished gold lustre (from Johnson Matthey), and Reusche glass enamels. Her pieces are hand built, and all of the surfaces – from the glaze through to the enamels – are hand painted. She uses mostly cobalt and copper for in-glaze painting.

The biscuit is fired to cone 06, the glaze to 04, the lustre to 017 and the enamels to 021. The enamelled pieces are then fired two or more times at 021 to build up the enamel layer; in the end, some of the pieces may have been fired up to seven or eight times. The most common total number of firings, however, is five.

Combined and other techniques

Marshall Colman, in addition to a range of maiolica tableware, also makes individual narrative pieces. These are particularly interesting for the way in which they combine decorative processes to achieve a greater level of complexity. Colman works on a sintered glaze, as this gives the hard surface which is favoured by his techniques.

> My narratives are paintings in three dimensions on a ceramic surface, in the tradition of the heroic portraits on English Delft and Italian *istoriato*

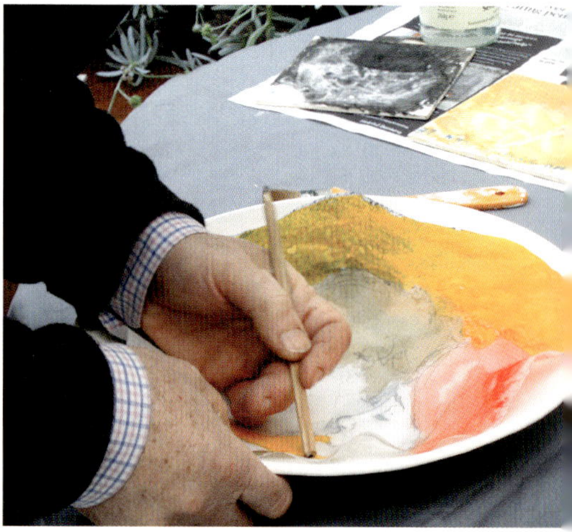

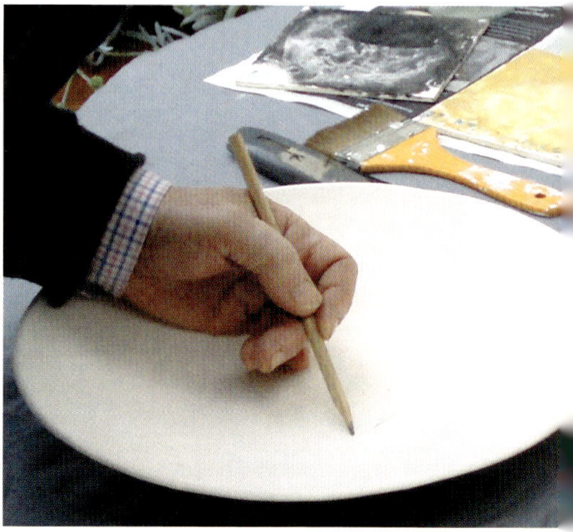

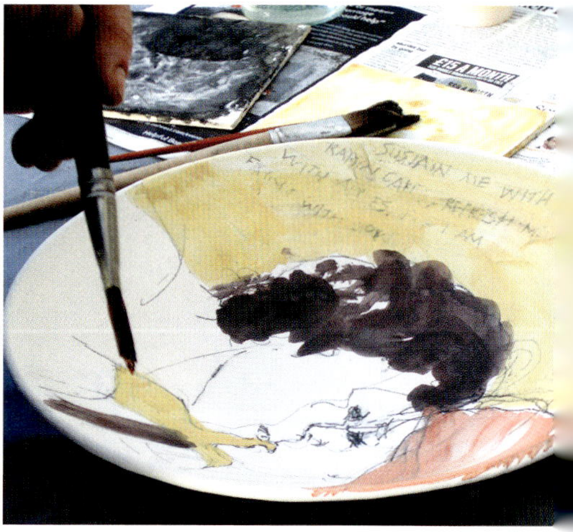

RIGHT, FROM TOP The image is transferred by rubbing through the design, which has been drawn with soft pencil on the back of the paper.

Sketching in the design in more detail with a lead pencil, which will burn out in the final firing.

Putting on washes of underglaze colours.

maiolica. I was captivated by the narrative ceramics in the Museum of Medieval and Modern Art in Arezzo, which claims to have the largest collection of *istoriato* work in Italy. Most of the museum's painted dishes illustrate Classical themes. I am currently doing illustrations of the Hebrew Bible. Tin glaze is a great example of cultural diffusion, carried by potters from the Middle East to Spain, Italy, the Netherlands, France and England – constantly changing, yet linked to tradition. I aim to make something completely modern, but with references to the past.

The designs use a mixture of commercial stains which give bright colours, and oxides which merge with the glaze in a more satisfactory way and give a better surface texture. The narratives require a wide palette, but typically each piece uses only four or five colours. Designs are applied in washes using wax resist, paper masks, sgraffito and underglaze pencil. On each narrative piece, I use a wider range of techniques than on the tableware to produce a richer and more complex image. The glaze on the narrative pieces is sintered – this stabilises it, but leaves it rough enough to be drawn on. I sketch the design with a lead pencil, brush on the oxides, and then draw the lines with an underglaze pencil last of all.

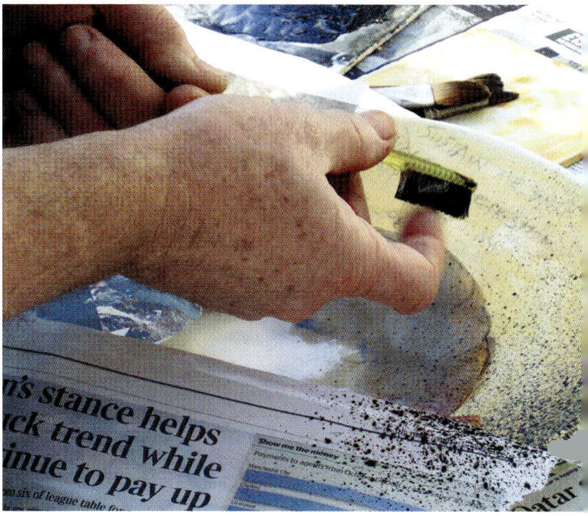

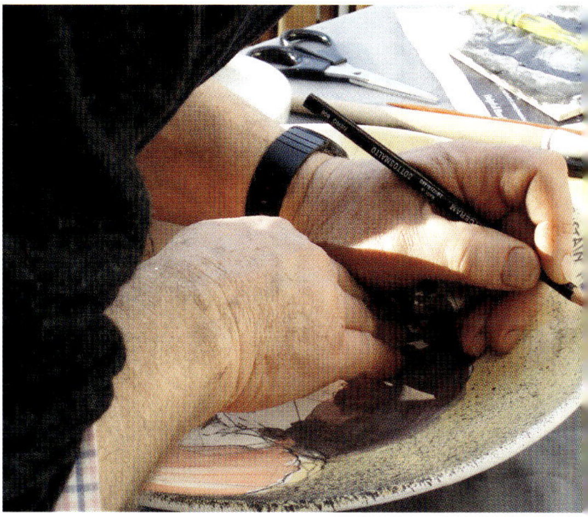

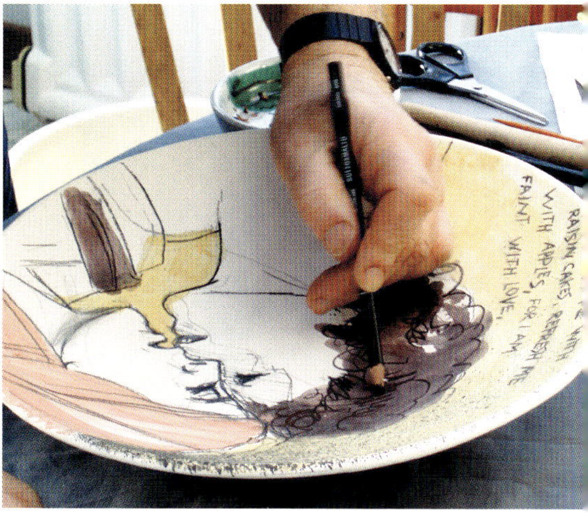

RIGHT, FROM TOP Adding some texture by spattering oxides over part of the design with a brush, the remainder masked with paper.

Adding the lettering in underglaze pencil.

Completing the drawing in underglaze pencil.

Photos courtesy of the artist.

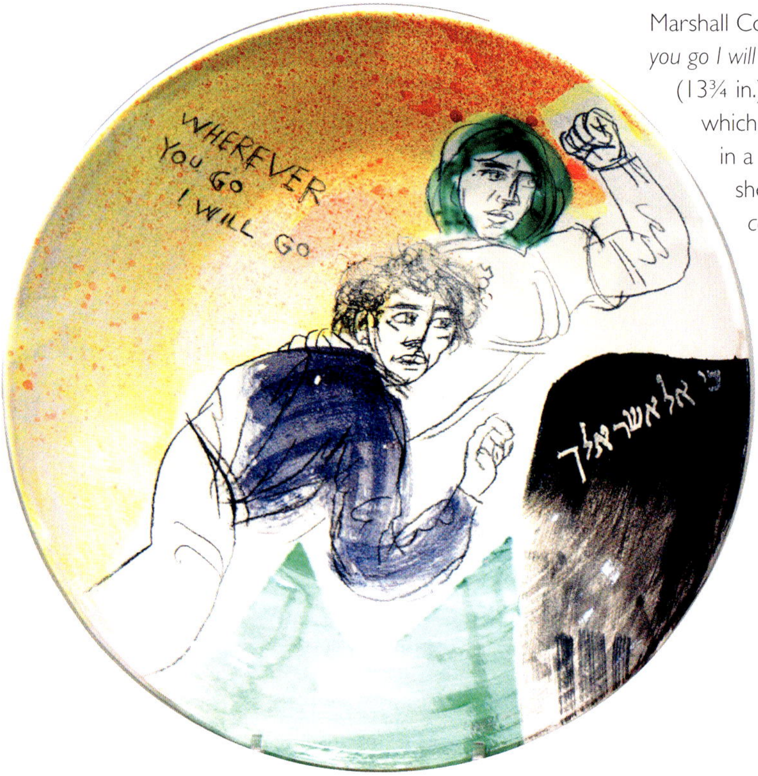

Marshall Colman, dish, *Wherever you go I will go*, 2009. Dia: 35 cm (13¾ in.). A finished piece which has been decorated in a similar way to that shown above. *Photo courtesy of the artist.*

Pieces are made in Valentine's standard red earthenware. Biscuit firing is to cone 06. The glaze is a lead-borosilicate base with tin and zirconium opacifiers, sintered at cone 017 before being fired up to cone 02.

Amy Cook uses complex decorative techniques – including application of slip at leatherhard stage, sgraffito and wax resist with tin glaze, and glaze-on-glaze. Her designs evolve from her love of wild flowers and plants, which goes back to her early childhood. She uses photography to capture details of buds, leaves and other details, and this then forms the basis for new surface treatments.

She makes a range of thrown and press-moulded vessels, including bowls, vases and cups. These use ivory stoneware and GT material (from Valentines), with each piece being deliberately distorted to reflect the natural imperfections of the flora that inspired them.

When the work is green, I use a spray gun to apply a black (cobalt, iron and manganese) slip in sweeping gestures across the pots. This is a careful process, as I want to engage with the nuances of the curves and distortions, emphasising the lighter and darker regions.

When my work is biscuit fired, I begin the process of decoration – by far the most time consuming and creative element of my making. I use a variety of oxide and stain-coloured tin glazes to create my detailed patterns, and the methods I use to create them

RIGHT *Cosmos Seed Head* vase by Amy Cook. Painting design in copper green tin glaze over biscuit-fired black slip surface.

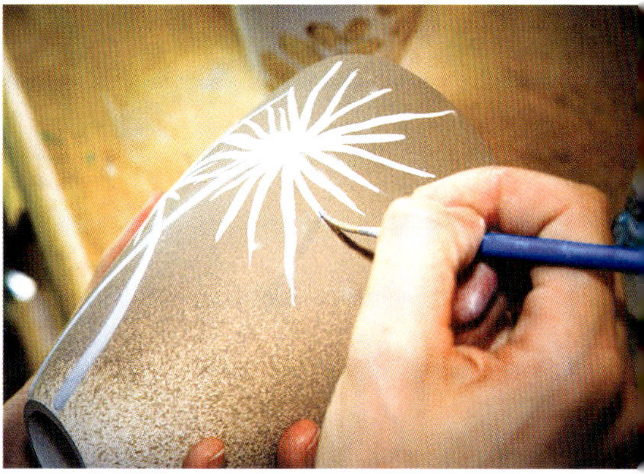

BELOW *Cosmos Seed Head* vases by Amy Cook, 2009. Ht (max): 16 cm (6¼ in.).

'The design was painted with copper tin glaze on a biscuit-fired black slip surface. Wax resist was then painted over the design and just over the edge so as to reveal a fine line of slip colour underneath. Finally, the whole piece was dipped in white tin glaze.'
Photos by Andrew Swarbrick.

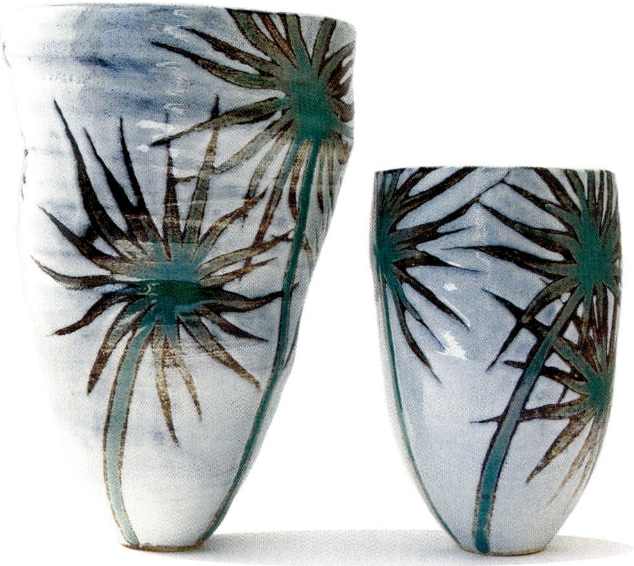

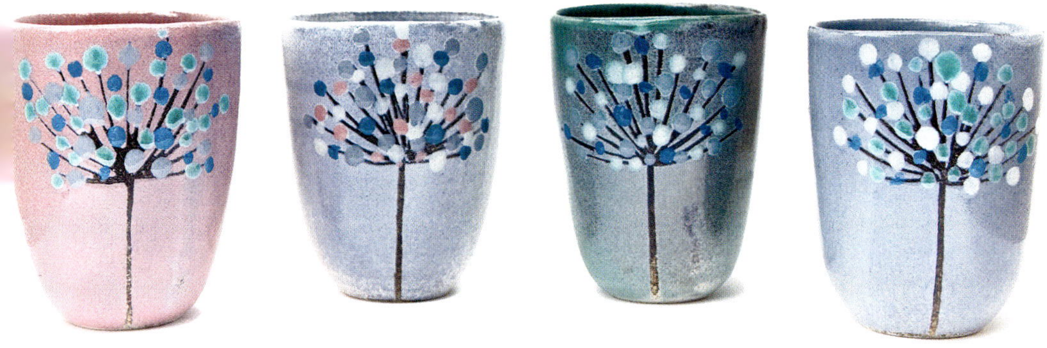

Cow Parsley Cups by Amy Cook. Ht: 8 cm (3 in.), Ivory stoneware, black slip, coloured tin glaze, sgraffito and painted design.

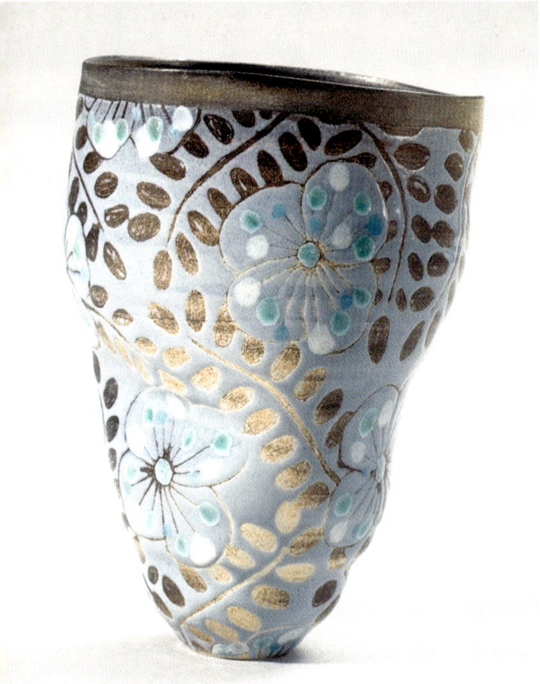

Blue Flower and Fern vase by Amy Cook, 2008. Ht: 18 cm (7 in.). Black slip has been applied at the leatherhard stage. The biscuit-fired piece was dipped in a blue-grey stained tin-glaze after applying wax resist to the rim. The leaf motif and lines were sgraffitoed through the glaze. Finally, white and copper-coloured tin glazes were painted on top. *Photo by Andrew Swarbrick.*

vary according to the type of piece that I'm making. With my smaller pieces, I either paint the design onto the pot with a colour before wax resisting and dip glazing, or I dip glaze, sgraffito, and then paint on the surface. Often, I will slightly adapt a technique for a piece or design, and am constantly evolving my methods. Biscuit firing is to 1000°C (1832°F), glaze firing to 1140°C (2084°F).

Morgen Hall also uses slips at the leatherhard stage, but in combination with intricately cut stencils, latex resist and slip trailing. The cobalt blue slip breaks through, but is softened by the tin glaze. Using slip rather than glaze stains allows for crisp-edged stencil patterns, as well as the tactile raised surfaces of slip-trailed marks.

The strong forms of Hall's contemporary domestic pieces bear witness to the influence of fine 18th century Staffordshire tableware. Food connections are essential; most of the pieces are specifically designed and inspired by the food for which they are intended. Surface designs are sourced from food-related shapes and patterns in fruits, vegetables and leaves. Vinyl stencils are made using a computer

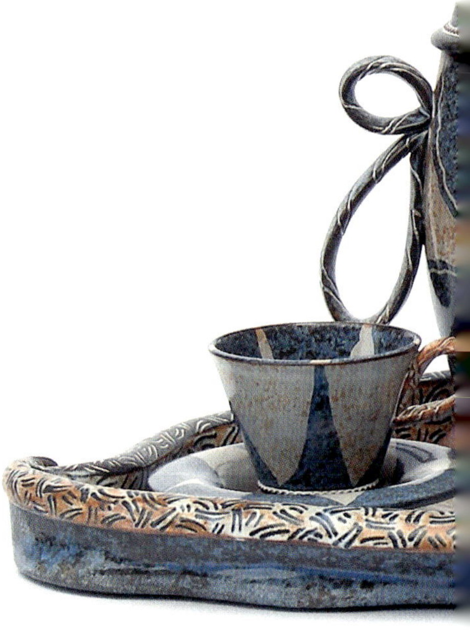

generated image on a plotter-cutter, and rubber stencils are also used to give an embossed image. Hall uses Valentine's Smooth Red Earthenware 120s mesh, with biscuit firing to 1000°C (1832°F). Prior to glaze firing, a rutile-based, mustard coloured glaze stain is applied on top of the white tin glaze. Glaze firing is to 1110°C (2030°F).

Morgen Hall glaze recipe
(cone 02, based on an Alan Caiger-Smith recipe)

Lead Bisilicate	56
Flint	8
Cornish stone	10
Standard borax frit	8
Zinc oxide	4
Tin oxide	8
Lithium carbonate	2

Blue slip (applied to leatherhard pot)

Valentine's red earthenware clay	60
Ball clay	40
Cobalt oxide	7–8%
Red iron oxide	2%

(Each new batch of slip is tested and adjusted for colour, with more iron oxide added if the blue is too bright.)

Rutile glaze stain (sponged over the tin glaze)
by volume
1 part tin glaze
1 part rutile light
1 part egg yolk yellow commercial glaze stain

Coffee Cabaret Set by Morgen Hall, 2006. L: 60 cm (23½ in.), ht (coffee pot): 31 cm (12¼ in.). *Photo courtesy of the artist.*

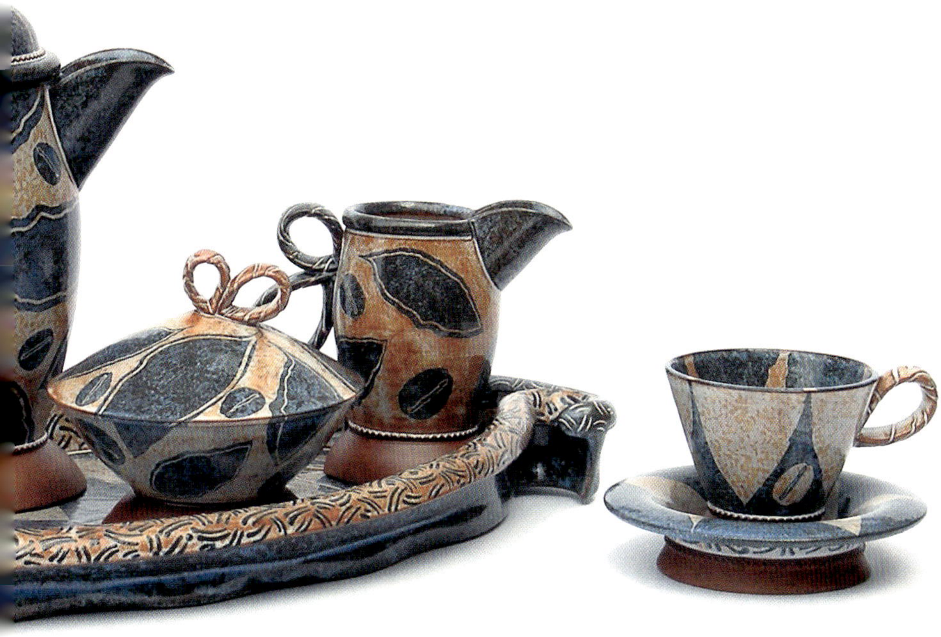

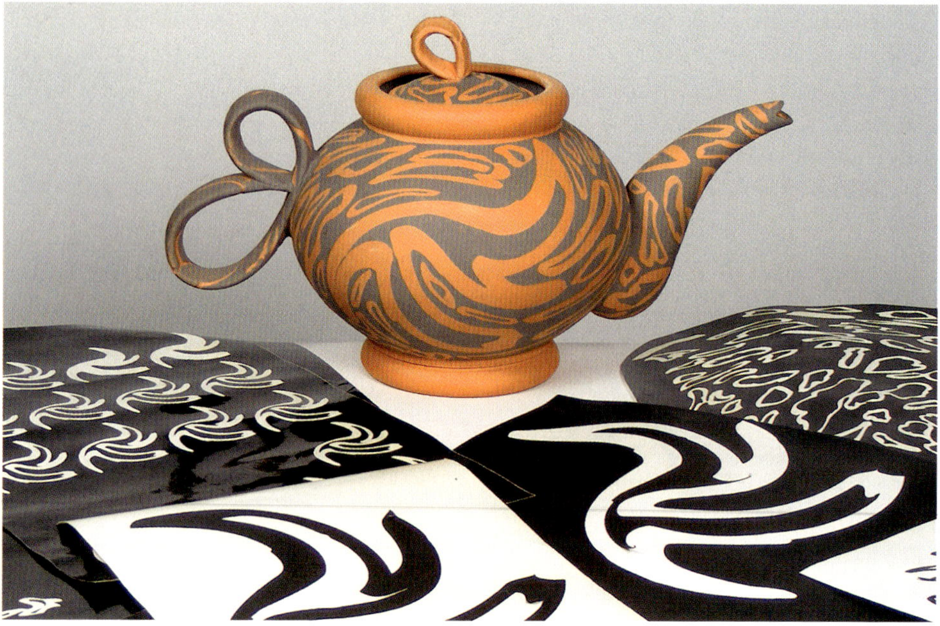

Biscuit-fired teapot with vinyl stencils of Darjeeling tea leaf patterns, by Morgen Hall. The stencils were made from a scanned image of tea leaves, manipulated using Photoshop, Illustrator and CADCAM software and cut using a plotter-cutter. The grey colour is the cobalt slip which will fire blue on the finished piece. *Photo courtesy of the artist.*

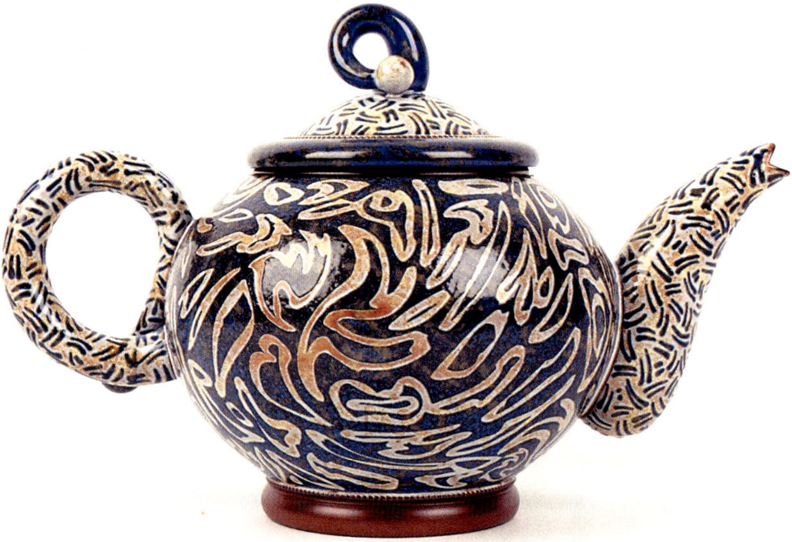

Teapot with Darjeeling tea leaf patterns, by Morgen Hall, 2005. Ht: 19 cm (7½ in.). *Photo courtesy of the artist.*

Lisa Katzenstein uses a wide variety of techniques and processes in her work: wax resist, inlay, sgraffito and painting all contribute to the particular detailed, layered effects which are characteristic of her pieces. Carrying these out on a sintered surface is central to the achievement of these effects.

Katzenstein describes her work as tin-glazed earthenware which 'happen to be pots'. Her simple, distinctive vase forms are constructed to look like sheets of paper which have been twisted around to form counter-balanced ovals and flat cylinders. As far as surface design goes, the main influence in her work comes from landscape painters, especially pre-war and post-war artists such as Graham Sutherland, Alan Reynolds and John Piper.

The pieces are slipcast using Potclays Semi-Porcelain casting slip. The models for her moulds are made out of hand-carved plaster. Bisque firing is to 1150°C (2102°F), and the glaze is sintered to 705°C (1300°F) to provide a firm, non powdery surface on which to work. This is then fired up to 1060–1070°C (1940–1958°F), with a one hour soak at top temperature.

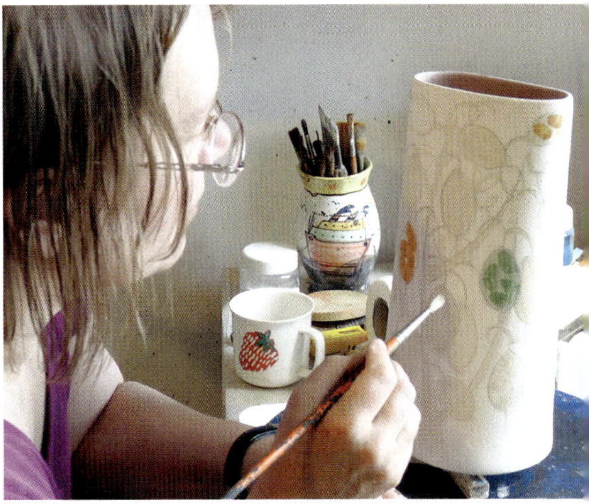

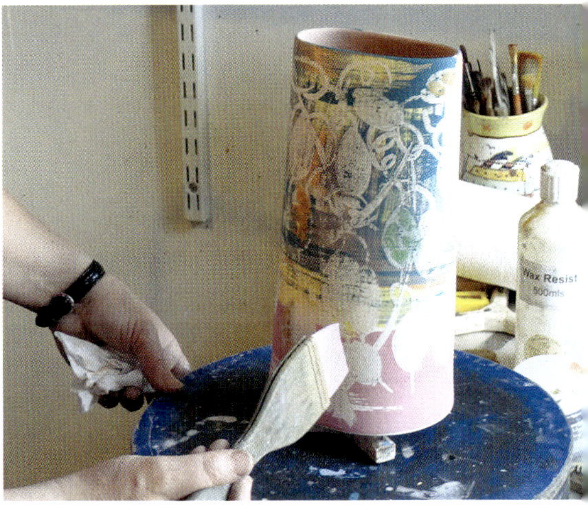

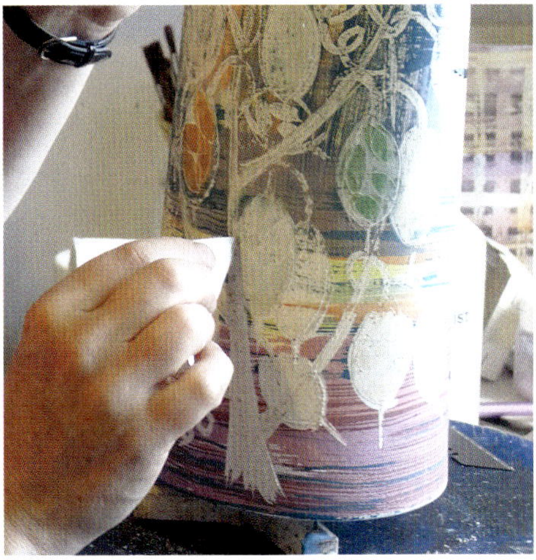

RIGHT, FROM TOP Wax emulsion resist is applied over the painted image of honesty.

Background colours are washed over the wax-resisted surface, working from lighter to darker colours using a hake brush.

Fine lines are scratched through the waxed areas, using the tip of a stanley blade.

Photos courtesy of the artist.

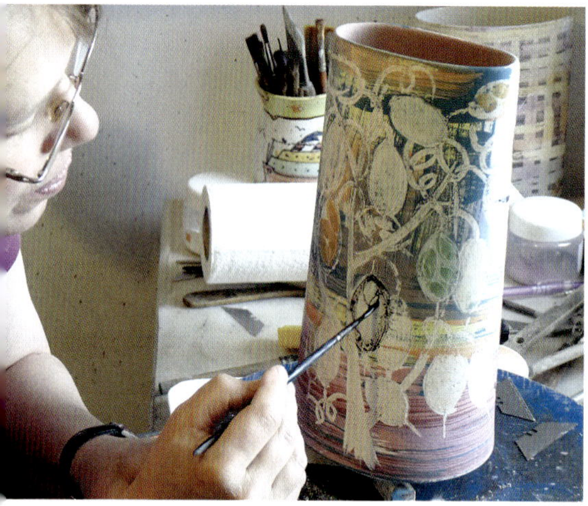

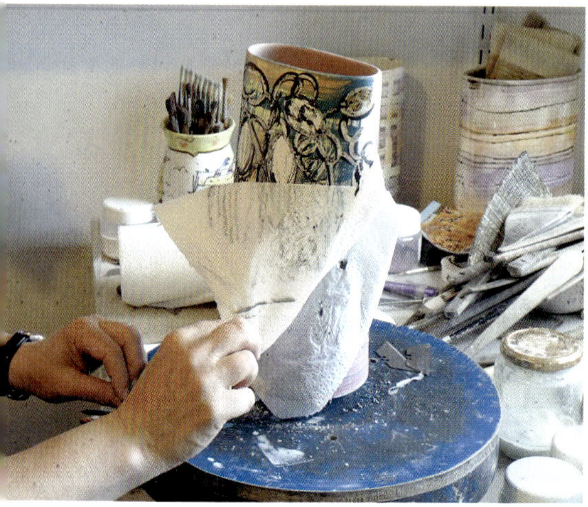

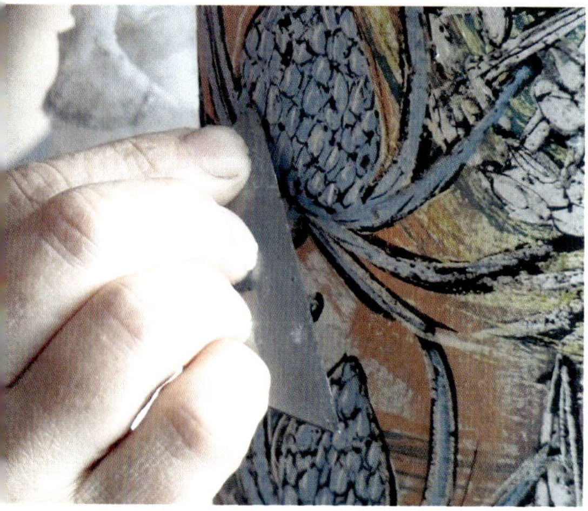

Lisa Katzenstein glaze recipes
(cone 04)

1	Lead bisilicate	62
	China clay	5
	Cornish stone	11
	Borax frit (P2955)	10
	Zinc oxide	2
	Tin oxide	10
2	Borax frit (P2955)	70
	Flint	5
	Ball clay	7.5
	China clay	7.5
	Zirconium silicate	10

For pigments, she uses glaze stains and underglazes mixed with water and a bit of clear glaze. For the lines, she uses an oxide mixture of cobalt oxide, manganese and cornish stone, sometimes using washes of cobalt carbonate as an 'under painting' to modify the brightness of the stains.

LEFT, FROM TOP The etched lines are inlaid with an oxide mixture of cobalt, manganese and Cornish stone, using a well-loaded brush.

Using paper towels, excess wax is removed to give cleaner lines.

Darker areas are highlighted by sgraffito back to the glaze.

OPPOSITE *Tall Twist vases* by Lisa Katzenstein, 2009. Ht: 36 cm (14¼ in.). Honesty and teasel designs.

Photos courtesy of the artist.

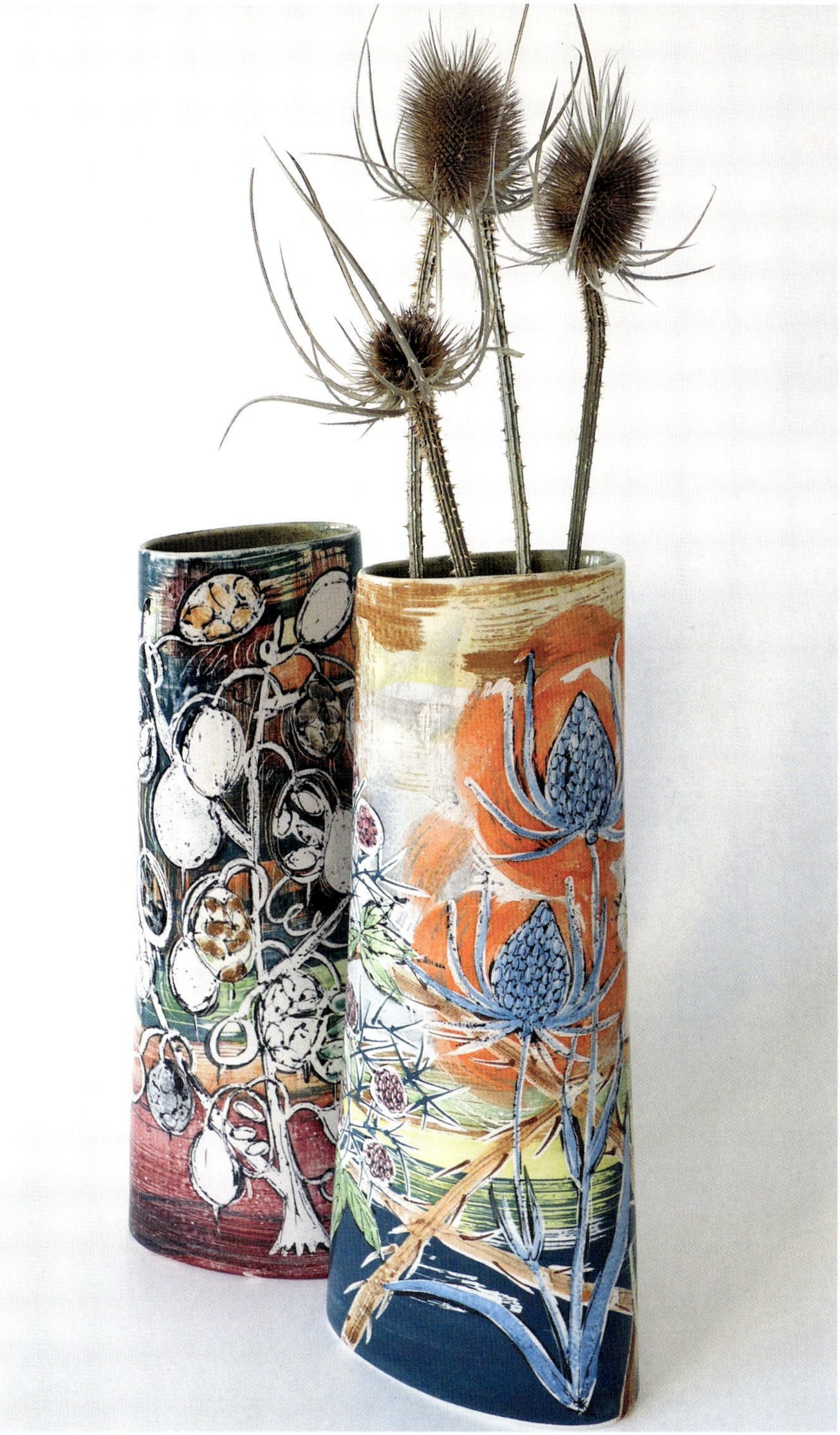

Maiolica on sculptural and relief surfaces

There is a long pedigree of tin glaze on sculptural and relief surfaces, dating back to 15th century architectural ceramics of Renaissance Italy. These notably include those of the della Robbia family, whose white relief portraits and religious groupings were framed by fruit and flowers in brightly coloured tin glazes.

Agalis Manessi's work celebrates this rich historical medium of sculptural maiolica through many diverse influences. Her subject matter is derived from portraits, figures and animal studies, either drawn directly from life or inspired by characters from paintings in museum collections. She strives for a poetic mastery through pictorial representation, trying to retain a freshness of palette that belies the difficulty of the process. Her modelled and coiled pieces are often based on cats and dogs – their animated, whimsical natures camouflaged within the painted surfaces, communicating silently yet eloquently the artist's message to the viewer.

Manessi uses red earthenware clay from Potclays, and P2023 tin glaze from Potterycrafts. Biscuit firing is to 1000°C (1832°F), and glaze firing to 1060–1070°C (1940–1958°F) with a 30 minute soak. All colourants are mixed with a little of the glaze and painted directly onto the unfired glaze surface.

> My palette is driven by what can be achieved through the intermixing of the oxides: cobalt for blues, copper and chrome for greens, the two used in combination to give turquoise, manganese for brown (everything from a pinky hue through to a rich purple brown sienna). Similarly,

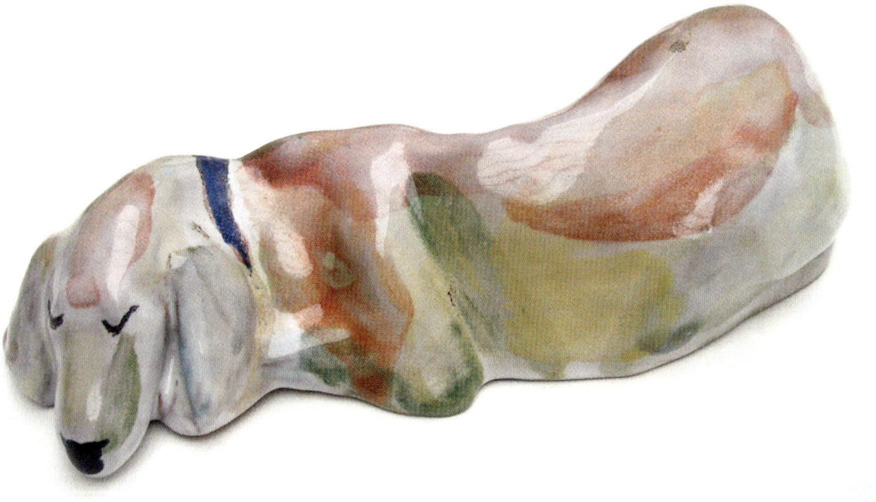

Sleeping Dog in Snow (after Franz Marc) by Agalis Manessi. 6 x 18 x 6 cm (2½ x 7 x 2½ in.).

'This piece was inspired by the painting *White Dog* by Franz Marc. The original palette is mostly blues and greens, but I wanted to explore a warmer range of colours. I think this dog is enjoying the sunshine – albeit in a snowy landscape!' *Photo by Rob Kesseler.*

RIGHT *Petite Fille* (after Samuel van Hoogstraten) by Agalis Manessi. 14 x 9 x 4 cm (5½ x 3½ x 1½ in.).

'I love looking at the 'little dog in the corner' in different paintings, and this piece came after several visits at the National Gallery – looking in particular at the work of Samuel van Hoogstraten. I called it *Petite fille*, as she seemed to have a girlie look.' *Photo by Rob Kesseler.*

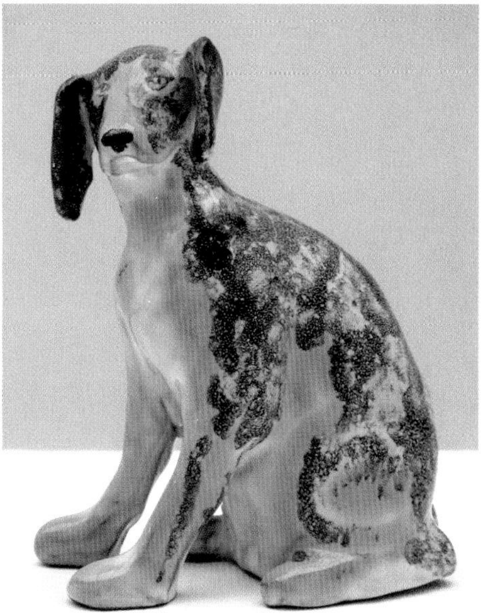

ferrous oxides, red iron, yellow ochre, crocus martis can all be used in combination to give a wide range of yellows, pinks, reddish browns and deep browns. This palette is supplemented with additional, industrially prepared stains to give a wider selection of stronger, purer colours that are difficult to achieve with oxides alone.

Back in the 1970's, a trip to Europe and the discovery of Caiger-Smith's book *Tin-glazed Pottery* opened **Dierdre Daw**'s eyes to the richness of the medium and its potential as a glaze for her relief and sculptural work. The endless possibilities for layers of colour using the maiolica technique over the red 'underpainting' of earthenware inspired her to work in a wide range of scale and formats: a two inch high cup; an entire room of tile floors and walls; 12-foot high sculptures. Colour, line and form work to convey nature, humans interacting with it, and her inner world.

The inspiration for the tulip vases came from a similar piece which I saw at the V&A from the times of the tulip mania in the Netherlands in the 1700s. The strange forms and the strange function, and the strange thought that a tulip bulb could cost the same as feeding a shipload of men for a year ... I wanted to try and combine the monumental tulip vase with the double-walled and pierced forms of Persian ware.

I build using coils, letting the work get hard enough to support any weight I build on top of it. I carve when the clay feels stiff, at the leatherhard stage. I then bisque to cone 07. Next, I dip, pour and brush the white maiolica glaze on to the pieces, and brush on top (using watercolour and sumi brushes) various Ferro, Mason, and Degussa stains, straight oxides, and carbonates with about 50% Ferro Frit #3124.

Besides using water as a vehicle, I squirt a CMC solution into my colours to get the proper 'drag' on the brush. To make this, I use about 100 grams of CMC to 4 litres of hot water, and then shake this before letting it stand overnight. I like to layer the transparent overglaze colours,

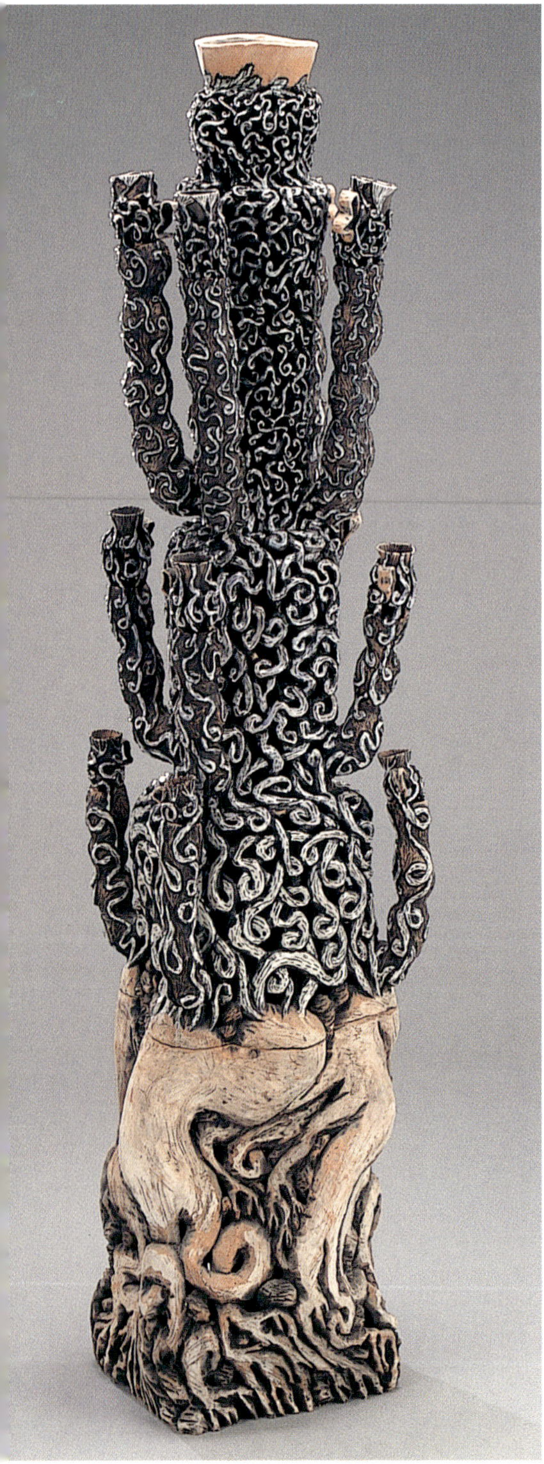

and have been using experimental textured glazes as well as terra sigillata – all fired to cone 04.

Val Cushing via Andrea Gill's maiolica – with tweaks (cone 04)

Frit 3124	65.75
Kona F-4 feldspar	17.14
Edgar's plastic kaolin	10.82
Nepheline syenite	6.29

plus

Tin oxide	7%
Superpax	7%
Bentonite	2%
Veegum T	0.5%
Golden brown stain	0.25%

LEFT Carved, double-walled tulip vase, by Deirdre Daw, 1995. Ht: 160 cm (63 in.). Detail below. *Photo by Koichro Hayashi, San Francisco.*

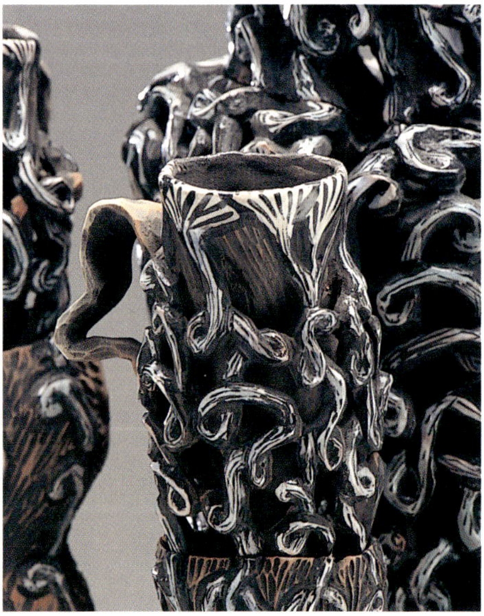

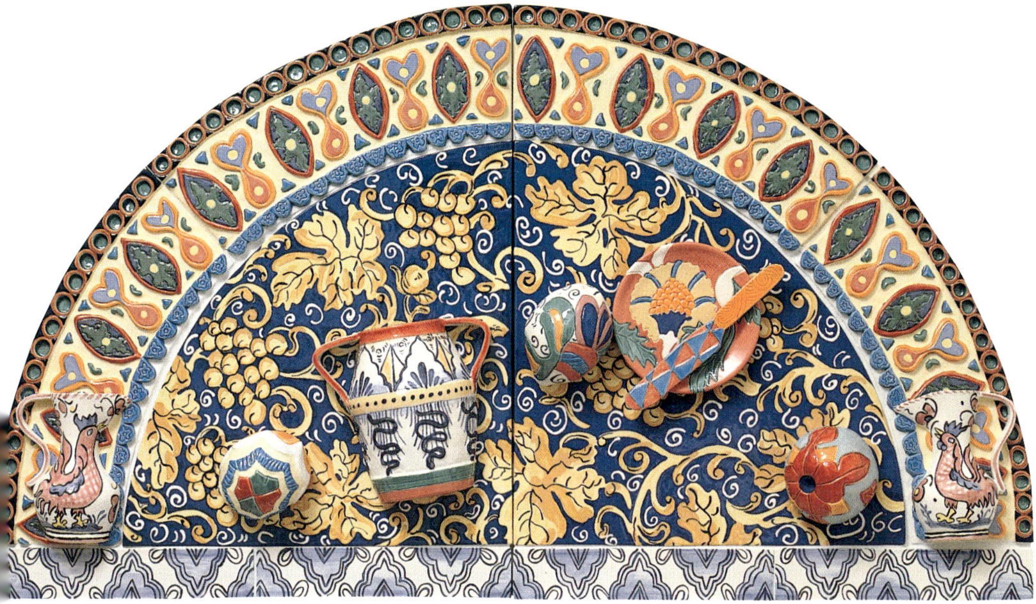

ABOVE *Orvieto Red Rooster* lunette by Karen Koblitz, 1994. 105.4 × 58.4 × 14 cm (41½ × 23 × 5½ in.). Renwick Gallery, Smithsonian American Art Museum, Washington D.C. *Photo by Susan Einstein.*

This is one of a series of four lunette works inspired by the ceramic work of the Della Robbia family, with references to both Italian architecture and traditional maiolica designs and colour palettes. It is made of white earthenware using handbuilding, slipcasting and thrown elements, with the vibrant colours and classic motifs being indebted to the Italian maiolica tradition. In-glaze decorated white maiolica can be seen in certain areas of the piece. Other areas are underglaze-painted with a transparent glaze on top.

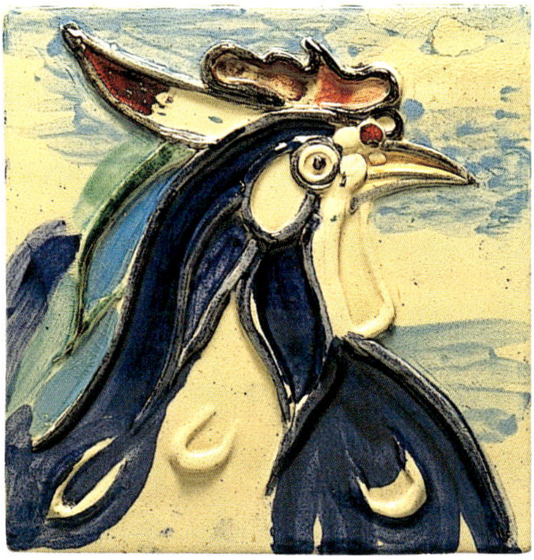

William Newland, test tile for a large mural, showing the *cuenca* technique of raised clay cloisonné walls separating the colours. *Photo by Douglas Cape.*

Chapter 4
Troubleshooting

Problems with lead and borax frit-based glazes

Problems have recently been brought to light regarding the behaviour of glazes containing lead bisilicate and borax frits. These issues include poor adhesion, cracking of raw glaze, reduced colour response, over-glossy finish and the shelling off of glaze from rims. When the glaze is freshly mixed up, it is usually problem free – over time, however, it 'goes off', and the above faults start to occur.

The problems appear to be related to the preparation of the frits themselves which are now mostly dry-milled in Spain and Portugal. This process leads to a very fine particle size, and is responsible for the gradual break-down of the glaze, causing increased solubility, higher raw shrinkage and other associated problems. The Stoke-on-Trent method of preparation is wet-milling, which results in a coarser and more stable particle size.

If your glaze has been problematic, make enquiries to your suppliers about the sources of their frits. According to Potclays, their lead and borax frits are still wet-milled, and therefore less likely to break down. Many other suppliers appear to stock only the dry-milled imported variety, but the wet-milled version is preferable.

Colours running

This issue can be caused by a number of factors:

- The glaze could have been applied too thickly
- The glaze may have 'curtained' during the glazing process
- The firing temperature may be too high – if this is the case, fire to the next cone down or stiffen up the glaze with 5–10% china clay
- The pigments may be too concentrated – cobalt and copper are strong fluxes, and could either be applied more thinly or balanced with the addition of some china clay (1:1 by volume).

Rough and blistered colours

This is caused by the refractory nature of certain oxides and stains, e.g. rutile and nickel oxide, and red, yellow, orange, green and quite a few other stains. These will require increased additions of either frit or glaze to help fusion. Another cause may be that stronger oxides such as cobalt, copper and manganese, have been applied too thickly, and become oversaturated and rough to the touch.

Glaze crawling

Maiolica glazes are viscous in nature, and as such are prone to crawling. This can happen if the glaze application is too thick, but the problem can normally be resolved as the glaze, on drying, will crack like dried mud. If this happens, wash off the glaze and start again.

In some places – such as where handles join bodies – glaze will collect and form cracks. To combat this, either reduce glaze absorption by painting water on to these areas prior to glazing, or rub over the cracks prior to firing. Application of over-watery colours can also lift the glaze and lead to crawling.

Glaze crazing

Crazing can occur because of a poor glaze-body fit, and is most likely to happen if the clay body is under-fired or if the glaze is applied too thickly. Thermal shock and absorption of moisture over time can also cause delayed crazing. Glazes containing alkaline frit are more likely to craze because of their high coefficient of expansion.

To combat the last issue, substitute borax frit, with its lower coefficient of expansion, for all or part of the alkaline frit. The addition of 5–10% flint or china clay to the glaze can also help. Alternatively, firing to a higher temperature will usually create greater contraction in the body, thus putting the glaze under a higher degree of compression and inhibiting the crazing process.

Porosity

All earthenware remains porous to a greater or lesser degree, even after glaze firing. This can pose problems for teapots, jugs, vases or any other vessel which is destined to hold liquids. Glazing pieces all over and firing them on stilts, or wiping glaze from bases to leave a thin film of glaze will help considerably.

Glaze pinholing or white-spotting

This is frequently caused by the insufficient clearing of gases such as carbon and sulphur in the biscuit firing. These later escape through the glaze, causing pinholing and/or white-spotting. To resolve the issue, biscuit firing should be taken slowly and never at a greater rate than 100°C (212°F) per hour. A slightly higher biscuit firing or a longer soak at top temperature will also allow for better gas clearance.

Pinholes can also be caused by air-pockets in the clay, particularly on turned areas where any grog has been brought to the surface. These areas should be compressed and smoothed after turning, either with a finger or a kidney.

Dunting

Dunting is most often caused by uneven body thicknesses,pieces only being glazed on one side, poor general construction, or the pooling of glaze in thin-walled areas. All of these problems create extra stresses on the body when it is expanding and contracting during the firing and cooling processes. To prevent dunting, therefore, slow firing and cooling is vital for large and/or potentially vulnerable pieces.

For further information on this and any other glaze faults, please refer to Harry Fraser's book, *Glaze Faults and their Remedies.*

Additional glaze recipes

Lead-based glazes

'European' glaze (cone 03–02)
Recipe from Nigel Wood

Lead bisilicate	71
China clay	13
Quartz	5
Tin oxide	11
Bentonite	2

L1 (cone 06–04)
A reliable lower temperature glaze

Lead bisilicate	80
China clay	10
Tin oxide	10

L2 (cone 03–02)
Excellent general purpose glaze

Lead bisilicate	75
Cornish stone	10
China clay	5
Tin oxide	10

LB2 (cone 03)
Soft milky high zinc glaze, good with cobalt blues – can appear quite crystalline. This is adapted from a recipe by Alan Caiger-Smith.

Lead bisilicate	56
Standard borax frit	8
Cornish stone	10
Flint	8
Zinc oxide	8
Tin oxide	10
China clay	5

LB4 (cone 02)
An excellent general purpose tin glaze, good for all colours – based on an original glaze by Alan Caiger-Smith. If greater opacity is required, substitute zircon-borax frit for half of the borax frit amount.

Lead bisilicate	61
Standard borax frit	9
Cornish stone	15
China clay	6
Zinc oxide	2
Zirconium silicate	7
Tin oxide	8
Bentonite	2

LB5 (cone 02)
A creamy satin glaze, breaking orange at higher temperatures or where thinly applied on a red body.

Lead bisilicate	61
Zircon-borax frit	9
Cornish stone	15
China clay	6
Tin oxide	4
Zirconium silicate	3
Titanium dioxide	3
Bentonite	2

Low lead glaze (cone 03–02)
Very low lead glaze recipe from Nigel Wood

High alkaline frit	37
Flint	34
Tin oxide	10
Whiting	5
Magnesium carbonate	4
Lead bisilicate	5
Bentonite	4

Lead-free glazes

Glaze A (cone 03)

Standard borax frit	55
High alkaline frit	23
China clay	15
Tin oxide	8
Zirconium silicate	6
Bentonite	2

Glaze B (cone 03–02)
High boron glaze from Nigel Wood

Calcium borate frit	76
Flint	10
Potash feldspar	12
Tin oxide	6
Bentonite	4

Liz Quackenbush glaze (cone 04)

Ferro frit 3124	140
Ball clay (om4)	14
Ferro frit 3110	20
Zircopax	20
Bentonite	10
Silica	35

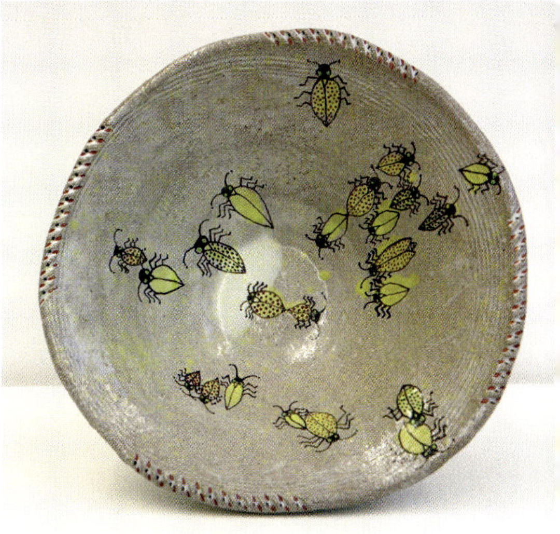

Beetles Bowl, by Hylton Nel, 2009. Dia: 21 cm (8¼ in.), ht: 9 cm (3½ in.). *Courtesy of Michael Stevenson, Cape Town.*

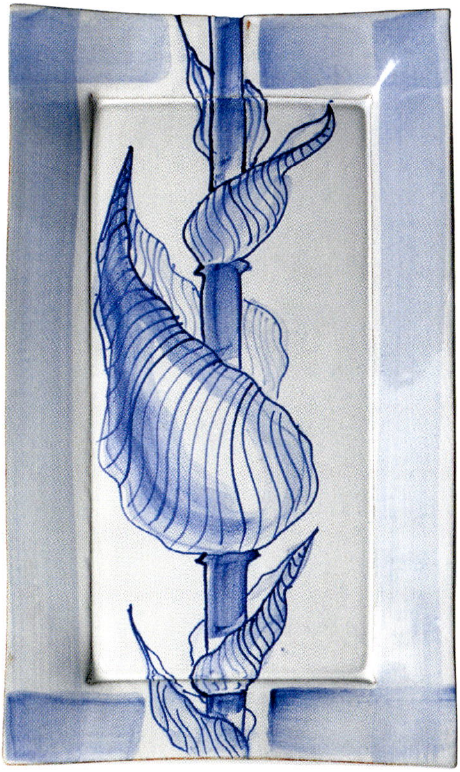

RIGHT *Canna Leaves*, dish by Daphne Carnegy, 2009. 34 × 21cm (13½ × 8¼ in.). Painted using varying strengths of cobalt oxide on glaze LB2. *Photo by Sussie Ahlburg.*

Technical information

Orton Pyrometric Cones Chart

(Courtesy of Edward Orton Jr. Ceramic Foundation)

8	2212	2280	2320				2277	2316			2372	
9	2235	2300	2336				2295	2332			2403	
10	2284	2345	2381				2340	2377			2426	
11	2322	2361	2399				2359	2394			2437	
12	2345	2383	2419				2379	2419			2471	2439
13		2428	2458				2410	2455				2460
13½		2466	2493									
14		2489	2523				2530	2491				2548
14½		2527	2568									
15		2583	2602				2595	2608				2606
15½		2617	2633									
16		2655	2687				2651	2683				2716
17		2694	2709				2691	2705				2754
18		2736	2746				2732	2743				2772
19		2772	2786				2768	2782				2806
20		2811	2824				2808	2820				2847
21		2851	2860				2847	2856				2883
23		2890	2898				2887	2894				2921
26							2892	2921				2950
27							2937	2961				2984
28							2946	2971				2995
29							2955	2993				3018
30							2977	3009				3029
31							3022	3054				3061
31½							3063	3088				3090
32							3103	3123				3123
32½							3124	3146				3135
33							3150	3166				3169
34							3195	3198				3205
35							3243	3243				3245
36							3268	3265				3279
37												3308
38												3362
39												3389
40												3425
41												3578
42												3659

8	1211	1249	1271				1247	1269			1300	
9	1224	1260	1280				1257	1278			1317	
10	1251	1285	1305				1282	1303			1330	
11	1272	1294	1315				1293	1312			1336	
12	1285	1306	1326				1304	1326			1355	1337
13		1331	1348				1321	1346				1349
13½		1352	1367									
14		1365	1384				1388	1366				1398
14½		1386	1409									
15		1417	1428				1424	1431				1430
15½		1436	1445									
16		1457	1475				1455	1473				1491
17		1479	1487				1477	1485				1512
18		1502	1508				1500	1506				1522
19		1522	1530				1520	1528				1541
20		1544	1551				1542	1549				1564
21		1566	1571				1564	1569				1584
23		1588	1592				1586	1590				1605
26							1589	1605				1621
27							1614	1627				1640
28							1619	1633				1646
29							1624	1645				1659
30							1636	1654				1665
31							1661	1679				1683
31½							1684	1698				1699
32							1706	1717				1717
32½							1718	1730				1724
33							1732	1741				1743
34							1757	1759				1763
35							1784	1784				1785
36							1798	1796				1804
37												1820
38												1850
39												1865
40												1885
41												1970
42												2015

Orton pyrometric cones chart (°F)

Cone Equivalent Temperatures (F)												
	Self Supporting Cones (1 3/4" mounting height)						Large Cones				Small (15/16" Height)	
	Regular			Iron Free			Regular		Iron Free		Regular	PCE
	Heating Rate (F/hour)						*Heating Rate (F/hour)*					
Cone	27	108	270	27	108	270	108	270	108	270	540	270
022	1049	1087	1094				N/A	N/A			1166	
021	1076	1112	1143				N/A	N/A			1189	
020	1125	1159	1180				N/A	N/A			1231	
019	1213	1252	1283				1249	1279			1333	
018	1267	1319	1353				1314	1350			1386	
017	1301	1360	1405				1357	1402			1443	
016	1368	1422	1465				1416	1461			1517	
015	1382	1456	1504				1450	1501			1549	
014	1395	1485	1540				1485	1537			1598	
013	1485	1539	1582				1539	1578			1616	
012	1549	1582	1620				1576	1616			1652	
011	1575	1607	1641				1603	1638			1679	
010	1636	1657	1679	1600	1627	1639	1648	1675	1623	1636	1686	
09	1665	1688	1706	1650	1686	1702	1683	1702	1683	1699	1751	
08	1692	1728	1753	1695	1735	1755	1728	1749	1733	1751	1801	
07	1764	1789	1809	1747	1780	1800	1783	1805	1778	1796	1846	
06	1798	1828	1855	1776	1816	1828	1823	1852	1816	1825	1873	
05½	1839	1859	1877	1814	1854	1870	1854	1873	1852	1868	1909	
05	1870	1888	1911	1855	1899	1915	1886	1915	1890	1911	1944	
04	1915	1945	1971	1909	1942	1956	1940	1958	1940	1953	2008	
03	1960	1987	2019	1951	1990	1999	1987	2014	1989	1996	2068	
02	1972	2016	2052	1983	2021	2039	2014	2048	2016	2035	2098	
01	1999	2046	2080	2014	2053	2073	2043	2079	2052	2070	2152	
1	2028	2079	2109	2046	2082	2098	2077	2109	2079	2095	2163	
2	2034	2088	2127				2088	2124			2174	
3	2039	2106	2138	2066	2109	2124	2106	2134	2104	2120	2185	
4	2086	2124	2161				2120	2158			2208	
5	2118	2167	2205				2163	2201			2230	
5½	2133	2197	2237				N/A	N/A			N/A	
6	2165	2232	2269				2228	2266			2291	
7	2194	2262	2295				2259	2291			2307	

Orton pyrometric cones chart (°C)

Cone Equivalent Temperatures (C)												
	Self Supporting Cones (1 3/4" mounting height)						Large Cones				Small (15/16" Height)	
	Regular			Iron Free			Regular		Iron Free		Regular	PCE
	Heating Rate (C/hour)						*Heating Rate (C/hour)*					
Cone	15	60	150	15	60	150	60	150	60	150	300	150
022	565	586	590				N/A	N/A			630	
021	580	600	617				N/A	N/A			643	
020	607	626	638				N/A	N/A			666	
019	656	678	695				676	693			723	
018	686	715	734				712	732			752	
017	705	738	763				736	761			784	
016	742	772	796				769	794			825	
015	750	791	818				788	816			843	
014	757	807	838				807	836			870	
013	807	837	861				837	859			880	
012	843	861	882				858	880			900	
011	857	875	894				873	892			915	
010	891	903	915	871	886	893	898	913	884	891	919	
09	907	920	930	899	919	928	917	928	917	926	955	
08	922	942	956	924	946	957	942	954	945	955	983	
07	962	976	987	953	971	982	973	985	970	980	1008	
06	981	998	1013	969	991	998	995	1011	991	996	1023	
05½	1004	1015	1025	990	1012	1021	1012	1023	1011	1020	1043	
05	1021	1031	1044	1013	1037	1046	1030	1046	1032	1044	1062	
04	1046	1063	1077	1043	1061	1069	1060	1070	1060	1067	1098	
03	1071	1086	1104	1066	1088	1093	1086	1101	1087	1091	1131	
02	1078	1102	1122	1084	1105	1115	1101	1120	1102	1113	1148	
01	1093	1119	1138	1101	1123	1134	1117	1137	1122	1132	1178	
1	1109	1137	1154	1119	1139	1148	1136	1154	1137	1146	1184	
2	1112	1142	1164				1142	1162			1190	
3	1115	1152	1170	1130	1154	1162	1152	1168	1151	1160	1196	
4	1141	1162	1183				1160	1181			1209	
5	1159	1186	1207				1184	1205			1221	
5½	1167	1203	1225				N/A	N/A			N/A	
6	1185	1222	1243				1220	1241			1255	
7	1201	1239	1257				1237	1255			1264	

Formulae of Ferro and Potclays Frits

(Courtesy of Potclays Ltd)

FRIT FORMULAE			
2261 Lead Bisilicate			% Analysis
PbO	0.086 Al_2O_3	1.850 SiO_2	PbO = 65.04 Al_2O_3 = 2.55 SiO_2 = 32.40
2262 Lead Sesquisilicate			
PbO	0.125 TiO_2	1.540 SiO_2	PbO = 68.52 TiO_2 = 3.07 SiO_2 = 28.41
2263 Standard Borax Frit			
0.033 K_2O 0.330 Na_2O 0.634 CaO 0.003 MgO	0.173 Al_2O_3	1.880 SiO_2 0.630 B_2O_3	K_2O = 1.33 Na_2O = 8.75 CaO = 15.22 MgO = 0.05 Al_2O_3 = 7.54 SiO_2 = 48.34 B_2O_3 = 18.76
2264 Soft Borax Frit	Formula not disclosed		
2265 H. T. Borax Frit			
0.033 K_2O 0.325 Na_2O 0.639 CaO 0.002 MgO	0.208 Al_2O_3	1.933 SiO_2 0.622 B_2O_3	K_2O = 1.28 Na_2O = 8.44 CaO = 14.68 MgO = 0.05 Al_2O_3 = 8.91 SiO_2 = 48.55 B_2O_3 = 18.09
2266 Ferro Crystal Frit			
0.064 K_2O 0.644 Na_2O 0.293 CaO	0.095 Al_2O_3	3.028 SiO_2 0.097 B_2O_3	K_2O = 2.31 Na_2O = 15.31 CaO = 6.29 Al_2O_3 = 3.71 SiO_2 = 69.77 B_2O_3 = 2.59
2268 Calcium Borate Frit			
1.000 CaO	0.097 Al_2O_3	0.609 SiO_2 1.500 B_2O_3	CaO = 27.10 Al_2O_3 = 4.77 SiO_2 = 17.68 B_2O_3 = 50.44
2269 Ferro Frit 3195			
0.315 Na_2O 0.685 CaO	0.399 Al_2O_3	2.748 SiO_2 1.113 B_2O_3	Na_2O = 5.72 CaO = 11.26 Al_2O_3 = 11.92 SiO_2 = 48.40 B_2O_3 = 22.70

Formulae of Ferro and Potclays Frits (continued)

FRIT FORMULAE			
2270 White Zircon Borax Frit			
0.414 Na_2O 0.061 ZnO 0.413 CaO 0.112 MgO	0.236 Al_2O_3	3.850 SiO_2 0.827 B_2O_3 0.426 ZrO_2	Na_2O = 6.06 ZnO = 1.17 CaO = 5.47 MgO = 1.06 Al_2O_3 = 5.67 SiO_2 = 54.60 B_2O_3 = 13.58 ZrO_2 = 12.38
2272 Ferro Frit 3124			
0.020 K_2O 0.289 Na_2O 0.691 CaO	0.271 Al_2O_3	2.544 SiO_2 0.551 B_2O_3	K_2O = 0.68 K_2O = 0.68 Na_2O = 6.46 CaO = 13.97 Al_2O_3 = 9.96 SiO_2 = 55.11 B_2O_3 = 13.82
2273 Ferro Frit 3134			
0.314 Na_2O 0.016 MgO 0.670 CaO		1.491 SiO_2 0.638 B_2O_3	Na_2O = 10.16 MgO = 0.34 CaO = 19.61 SiO_2 = 6.74 B_2O_3 = 23.16
2275 High Alkali Frit			
0.330 K_2O 0.500 Na_2O 0.170 CaO	0.100 Al_2O_3	1.500 SiO_2 0.100 B_2O_3	K_2O = 17.35 Na_2O = 17.46 CaO = 5.32 Al_2O_3 = 5.69 SiO_2 = 50.30 B_2O_3 = 3.88
2279 Low Expansion Frit			
0.176 Li_2O 0.324 CaO 0.173 ZnO 0.252 MgO	0.400 Al_2O_3	5.290 SiO_2 1.280 B_2O_3	Li_2O = 0.10 CaO = 3.60 ZnO = 3.30 MgO = 2.40 Al_2O_3 = 8.20 SiO_2 = 63.60 B_2O_3 = 17.80

The information given here is for guidance only, and whilst we believe it to be correct it should not be taken as a guarantee for any individual batch of material. Some slight variation may occur due to natural variations in raw materials.

Health and safety

The best policy with regard to health and safety in the studio is to adopt good habits and take effective precautions. There is often much hysteria associated with the toxicity or hazardousness of certain materials, but dealing with ceramic materials is analogous to the way we use household chemicals in our homes; if straightforward common sense prevails, then it is unlikely that ceramicists will be adversely affected.

Hazardous dust

Silica

Silica dust is without doubt the greatest hazard in the studio, and is present not only in clay, but also in all glazes through flint, china clay, ball clay, feldspars and frits. Exposure to silica dust over extended periods can lead to emphysema, tuberculosis, silicosis and pneumonia. It is the finest particles which are the most dangerous.

To guard against silica-related dangers:

- Minimise work with dry clay and dry glazes
- Wear a good quality dust mask if you have to work with dry clay, and also when rubbing or fettling dry glaze
- Always wet clean
- Wash overalls regularly.

Alumina

This is also present in all clays and the majority of earthenware glazes through the introduction of china clay, ball clay, feldspars and frits. As this is also hazardous, the same precautions outlined for silica should be observed.

Toxic materials

Of the substances most likely to be used in maiolica, the most toxic substances include compounds of the following:

Lead

Present in lead bisilicate, lead sesquisilicate and some pigments. Fritted lead is in theory insoluble in its raw state, but some precautions should still be taken. The fact that fritted lead is used in a glaze does not automatically mean that the fired glaze is safe, either, and any glazes and pigments containing lead need to be tested for lead release (see p.104 for contact details regarding testing).

Barium

Sometimes used in maiolica glazes to give smooth matt glazes and heightened colour response. Toxic both raw and fired.

Antimony

With lead, creates the 'Naples Yellow' of Italian maiolica.

Vanadium

Rarely used in maiolica, as highly refractory and a weak colourant. Not food safe at earthenware temperatures. Highly toxic in raw state.

Chromium

Present in many manufactured stains and underglaze colours. Also used to give pinks and reds with tin oxide in the presence of calcium.

Cadmium and selenium
Most often associated with high temperature yellows, oranges and reds.

Manganese
Commonly used in maiolica pigment mixtures. Toxic in its raw state, but not when fired.

Soluble salts
Sulphates, nitrates and chlorides of cobalt, copper, manganese, iron and chrome. Used for soft, suffused effects in maiolica.

Other toxic substances

Boric oxide
Present in frits.

Lithium carbonate
Sometimes used in maiolica glazes.

Potash
Present in frits and feldspars.

Zinc oxide
Frequently used in maiolica glazes.

Iron chromate
Used as a pigment.

COSHH (Control of Substances Hazardous to Health – OSHA in the USA) data is available from the manufacturers or suppliers of ceramic materials, usually free of charge, and is also often available on the internet. Material Safety Data Sheets (MSDS) can also be found online. These describe the level of toxicity associated with each oxide and the possible consequences of overexposure or absorption. Assessments for all glaze materials, colouring oxides and stains are available from suppliers, but as a matter of general principle, it is wise to observe the following precautions:

- Use a barrier cream to prevent cracked skin on hands, through which toxins could enter the body
- Wear surgical gloves when handling glazes and glaze materials
- Wear a mask to avoid breathing in toxic dust
- Wear overalls and wash them regularly.

Solubility

The degree of hazard associated with any toxic substance is not just dependent on what the substance is, but also on how soluble it is. The greater the solubility, the more easy it is for the body to absorb. Even materials in 'highly insoluble' forms (e.g. frits) can remain relatively toxic, and all precautions should be observed when handling such materials.

Insolubility in a material's raw state does not necessarily guarantee insolubility in a fired glaze. This makes finished products potentially dangerous for consumers – particularly when acids (e.g. fruit juices, salad dressing etc.) are likely to be used with the items. The most common dangers come from lead, barium and some colourants such as cadmium and nickel. Glazes and pigments should always be tested for metal release, especially for any wares destined to be used with food and drink.

Metal release is also affected by certain other factors:

- Copper oxide should never be used with a lead-based glaze on domestic ware, as it will increase the risk of metal release in the fired glaze by up to 100 times permissible levels.
- A glaze containing a combination of lead and borax or alkaline frits is less

acid resistant than one which is just based on a lead frit.

- Underfired glazes and pigments which are poorly glossed-over or are thick and/or metallic are more susceptible to acid attack.
- A higher silica content and higher glaze temperature will give a harder, more resistant glaze surface. Alumina and titania also assist in combating acid attack.

The general trend (following the example of the USA) is for glazes to become lead-free. This is sad in a way, as lead-based glazes have particular qualities which promote a lustrous and craze resistant surface. A lead-based glaze, correctly formulated and fired, can be perfectly safe for tableware, although this should always be confirmed through industrial testing.

Testing of glazes and colours

Metal release testing UK
CERAM
Queens Road
Penkhull
Stoke-on-Trent
Staffordshire
ST4 7LQ
Tel. 01782 764428
Tel. (UK customers) 0845 026 0902
Email: enquiries@ceram.com
www.ceram.com

Metal release testing USA
Brandywine Science Center, Inc.
204 Line Road
Kennett Square, PA 19348
Phone: 610-444-9850
Web site: http://www.bsclab.com/

Loring Laboratories Ltd.
629 Beaverdam Road N.E.
Calgary, AB
T2K 4W7
Canada
Tel: (403) 274-2777
www.loringlabs.net

Other consumer considerations

Crazed glazes on earthenware are not appropriate: as the bodies remain porous, liquids and food can get absorbed through the cracks in the glaze, from where they can promote bacterial activity.

Kilns and firing

Toxic fumes are given off in all firings, but particularly in glaze firings. These fumes include those given by sulphides, chlorides, fluorides and volatile materials such as antimony, boron, cadmium, selenium, lead, zinc and precious metals (in lustres and enamel firings).

Good ventilation and/or extraction is essential when firing a kiln. In a small studio space, it is a good idea to fire the kiln at night so that you are not present when the fumes are released.

List of suppliers

UK

Clays, glaze materials, stains etc.

W. G. Ball Ltd
Anchor Road,
Longton,
Stoke-on-Trent,
ST3 1JW
Tel: 01782 312286
www.wgball.com
(underglaze and on-glaze colours)

Ceramatech Ltd
Units 16 &17 Frontier Works,
33 Queen Street,
London, N17 8JA
Tel: 020 8885 4492
www.ceramatech.co.uk
(general supplies)

CTM
Unit 10A, Mill Park Industrial Estate,
White Cross Road,
Woodbury Salterton,
EX5 1EL
Tel: 01395 233077
www.ctmpotterssupplies.co.uk
(general supplies)

Potclays Ltd
Brickkiln Lane, Etruria
Stoke-on-Trent,
Staffordshire,
ST4 7BP
Tel: 01782 219816
www.potclays.co.uk
(general – including wet-milled lead and borax frits)

Potterycrafts Ltd
Campbell Road,
Stoke-on-Trent,
Staffordshire ST4 4ET
Tel: 01782 745000
www.potterycrafts.co.uk
(general – including Amaco gloss decorating colours)

Scarva Pottery Supplies
Unit 20,
Scarva Road Industrial Estate,
Banbridge, Co. Down,
Northern Ireland,
BT32 3QD
Tel: 0 (044) 28 406 69699
www.scarvapottery.com
(general – including Mason stains)

Valentine Clays Ltd
The Sliphouse
18-20 Chell Street
Hanley
Stoke-on-Trent
ST1 6BA
Tel: 01782 271200
www.valentineclays.co.uk
(mostly clays)

Soluble colourants

Abbey Chemicals
29 North River Road
Great Yarmouth
Norfolk NR30 1SH
www.abbey-chemicals.co.uk
(copper sulphate)

Garden centres: *iron sulphate*

Maplin shops: *iron chloride (used for etching circuit boards)*

Brushes

Jackson's Art Supplies (online)
1 Farleigh Place
London N16 7SX
Tel: 0844 499-8430
www.jacksonsart.co.uk

USA

Amaco
6060 Guion Road,
Indianapolis, IN 46254-1222
Tel: Toll free (800) 374-1600
www.amaco.com
(general – including majolica gloss decorating colours)

Axner Ceramic Supply
490 Kane Court
Oviedo, FL 32765
Tel: (407) 365-2600
Toll free (800) 843-7057
www.axner.com
(general supplies)

Laguna Clay Company
14400 Lomitas Avenue
City of Industry
CA 91746
Tel: Freephone (800) 4-LAGUNA
(626) 330-0631
www.lagunaclay.com

Mason Color Works Inc
PO Box 76
East Liverpool
Ohio 43920-5076
Tel: (330) 385-4400
www.masoncolor.com
(stains)

Mile-Hi Ceramics
77 Lipan
Denver, CO 80223
Tel: (303) 825-4570
www.milehiceramics.com

Standard Ceramic Supply Company
PO Box 16240
Pittsburgh
PA 15242-0240
Tel: (412) 276-6333
www.standardceramic.com
(general supplies)

Tuckers Pottery Supplies Inc.
15 West Pearce Street, Unit 7
Richmond Hill
Ontario, Canada L4B 1H6
Tel: (800) 304-6185
www.tuckerspottery.com

Practitioners' websites

Stanley Mace Andersen: www.pottersoftheroan.com/Andersen_Pottery.htm
Linda Arbuckle: http://lindaarbuckle.com/handouts
Molly Attrill: www.axisweb.org (artist no.1722)
Posey Bacopoulos: www.poseybacopoulos.com
Megan Bogonovich: www.meganbogonovich.com
Amy Cook: www.amycookdesign.co.uk
Daphne Carnegy: www.daphnecarnegy.com
Marshall Colman: www.marshallcolman.com
Steve Davis-Rosenbaum: www.darogallery.com
Philip Eglin: www.bmgallery.co.uk/eglin/eglin.htm
Morgen Hall: www.morgenhall.com
Mohamed Hamid: www.hamid-pottery.co.uk
Lisa Katzenstein: www.lisakatzenstein.co.uk
Phyllis Kloda: www.brockport.edu/art/faculty/pkloda.html
Karen Koblitz: www.karenkoblitz.com
Susannah Lints: www.lints100.com
Agalis Manessi: http://www.broadwayceramics.com/people/Agalis_Manessi/
Laurence McGowan: www.laurencemcgowan.co.uk
Hennie Meyer: www.studiopottery.co.uk
Hylton Nel: www.michaelstevenson.com
Farraday Newsome: www.indigostreetpottery.com
Matthias Ostermann: www.matthiasostermann.com
Walter Ostrom: www.walterostrom.com
Liz Quackenbush: www.artaxis.org/ceramics/quackenbush
Kari Radasch: www.kariradasch.com
Reptile: www.reptiletiles.co.uk
Kate Scott: www.katescottceramics.co.uk
Jessica Wall: www.jessicawallceramics.co.uk
Bronwyn Williams-Ellis: www.handmade-tiles.co.uk
Gloria Young: www.nzpotters.com/PottersPages

Bibliography

Caiger-Smith, Alan, *Lustre Pottery*, London (Faber and Faber, 1985); also in paperback (Herbert Press)
Caiger-Smith, Alan, *Tin-glaze Pottery in Europe and the Islamic World*, London (Faber and Faber, 1973)
Carnegy, Daphne, *Tin-glazed Earthenware*, London (A & C Black, 1993)
Fraser, Harry, *Glaze Faults and their Remedies*, London (A & C Black, 1986)
Girel, J, Haby, R, Jacquinot, J, *Les Faiences de Slavik et Claude Palley*, Neuilly en Sancerre (Edition AACSP, 2008)
Hamer, Frank and Janet, *The Potter's Dictionary of Materials and Techniques*, Fifth edition, London (A & C Black, 2004), Philadelphia (University of Pennsylvania Press)
Ostermann, Matthias, *The New Maiolica*, London (A & C Black, 1999)
Shaw, Kenneth, *Ceramic Colours and Pottery Decoration*, London (Faber and Faber, 1962)
Stevenson, Michael, *Hylton Nel*, London (The Fine Art Society, 2003), Cape Town (Michael Stevenson Contemporary)

Index